YORK NOTES

Richard III

William Shakespeare

Note by Rebecca Warren

 Longman

 York Press

Exterior picture of the Globe Theatre reproduced by permission of the
Raymond Mander and Joe Mitchenson Theatre Collection
Reconstruction of the Globe Theatre Interior reprinted from Hodges:
The Globe Restored (1968) by permission of Oxford University Press

YORK PRESS
322 Old Brompton Road, London SW5 9JH

PEARSON EDUCATION LIMITED
Edinburgh Gate, Harlow,
Essex CM20 2JE, United Kingdom
Associated companies, branches and representatives throughout the world

First published 2001
Eighth impression 2007

ISBN: 978-0-582-43143-0

Designed by Vicki Pacey
Phototypeset by Gem Graphics, Trenance, Mawgan Porth, Cornwall
Colour reproduction and film output by Spectrum Colour
Produced by Pearson Education Asia Limited, Hong Kong

CONTENTS

PART ONE

INTRODUCTION

HOW TO STUDY A PLAY

Studying on your own requires self-discipline and a carefully thought-out work plan in order to be effective.

- Drama is a special kind of writing (the technical term is 'genre') because it needs a performance in the theatre to arrive at a full interpretation of its meaning. Try to imagine that you are a member of the audience when reading the play. Think about how it could be presented on the stage, not just about the words on the page.

- Drama is often about conflict of some sort (which may be below the surface). Identify the conflicts in the play and you will be close to identifying the large ideas or themes which bind all the parts together.

- Make careful notes on themes, character, plot and any **sub-plots** of the play.

- Why do you like or dislike the characters in the play? How do your feelings towards them develop and change?

- Playwrights find non-realistic ways of allowing an audience to see into the minds and motives of their characters, for example **soliloquy, aside** or music. Consider how such dramatic devices are used in the play.

- Think of the playwright writing the play. Why were these particular arrangements of events, characters and speeches chosen?

- Cite exact sources for all quotations, whether from the text itself or from critical commentaries. Wherever possible find your own examples from the play to back up your own opinions.

- Always express your ideas in your own words.

This York Note offers an introduction to *Richard III* and cannot substitute for close reading of the text and the study of secondary sources.

This play tells the sensational story of one of England's most notorious and vilified murderers, the demon king, Richard III. To this day, the last Plantagenet monarch exerts a powerful hold on the nation's imagination. Detractors and apologists continue to debate his character and his crimes, inevitably focusing on the mysterious circumstances that surround the deaths of Edward IV's unfortunate sons. Who has not heard the tragic tale of the innocent princes put to death in the Tower of London by their wicked, crookbacked uncle? Our enduring fascination with Richard and his reign is largely due to the theatrical brilliance of Shakespeare's portrait of his villain-hero.

It is easy to see why this dramatist's Richard has etched himself onto the national consciousness. Grotesque, bloody and terrifying, Shakespeare's villain is also witty, insouciant and seductive. The mixture makes for an irresistible portrait of implacable and energetic wickedness. This anti-hero dominates the stage in a way that few other evil – or virtuous – characters in the plays of the period can match. We are disarmed in the very first scene when Richard declares his subversive intentions. Thereafter we find ourselves mesmerised as he disposes – effortlessly – of one victim after another. Richard is entertaining in a way that Iago and Macbeth, Shakespeare's other magnificent villains, never are. All three chill our blood, but Richard also makes us laugh. He jokes. He plays with words. He turns to us and demands our attention through his use of **asides** and **soliloquies**. Because he is so exuberant and pleased with himself, and so in command as he pursues the crown, we are forced to admire Gloucester, even though his actions are deplorable.

This is a play about power as well as evil. Throughout his **history plays**, which cover the reigns of King John and then Richard II to Henry VIII, Shakespeare offers a unique portrait of the English elite and their shifting fortunes. Conflict lies at the heart of the history plays, which are concerned with the nature and responsibilities of kingship. Brothers, fathers and sons fight with one another for power, and for control of the crown. In the *Henry VI* trilogy in particular, men become embroiled in cycles of sin and retribution that reveal the moral dimensions and purposes of the genre. In *Richard III* the dramatist explores an idea that particularly intrigued him: what happens when the monarch is an individualistic tyrant who deserves to be overthrown?

What happens when evil goes unchecked? These were topical themes Shakespeare would return to in *Macbeth* and *King Lear*.

For a modern audience, watching the play with an understanding of the horrors perpetrated by a number of twentieth-century dictators, *Richard III* is intriguing because it seems to offer an ambiguous message about the nature of power and evil. Although Shakespeare suggests that God has control of human affairs, his villain also exercises his own free will when he damns himself. He chooses to be bad, and revels in his own evil. Even in his most desperate hour, Richard refuses to give in and accept the codes of the society he lives in, and he dies a valiant death on the battlefield. There is something heroic about his godless stoicism. All these details make us queasy. We are forced to acknowledge the allure and power of self-conscious wickedness. It is still deeply shocking to realise that one man's evil is capable of throwing a nation into chaos. The vulnerability of the nation is a theme that lies at the heart of the history plays.

Richard III was topical in its own time for another reason. It deals with the issue of succession, which was particularly contentious during Queen Elizabeth I's reign. Elizabeth refused to marry and thereby secure the succession by providing an heir. There were also plots to usurp her, two of the most famous involving Mary Queen of Scots and the Earl of Essex. Elizabeth, like Richard, could never be absolutely sure that she would not be challenged.

Richard III is the end of one historical story, the Wars of the Roses, which are depicted in *1–3 Henry VI*. Shakespeare's sources suggested that Richard's reign brought an end to the destructive chain of events set in motion when Richard II was usurped by Henry Bolingbroke. Richard III was therefore an extremely important figure in English history; without him, according to Renaissance historians, there would have been no Tudor dynasty. In Shakespeare's play the last Yorkist king is portrayed as God's scourge, sent to punish England. When he has done this job he is replaced by the Lancastrian Richmond, who promises to bring peace and prosperity to the beleaguered realm. Henry VII was the first Tudor monarch, under whose successors the dramatist lived and worked. One of the key issues when reading the play, then, is to consider the way in which Shakespeare chooses to portray the house of Tudor and its rise to power. It is easy to be distracted by Richard's character, but in order to understand the political and historical meanings of the play fully, it is necessary to look closely at his adversary too.

Modern readers will be intrigued by the presentation of the female characters in this play. Often history plays seem to focus almost exclusively on the fortunes of men, and the women are incidental to the action. This is not quite the case in *Richard III*, which includes a particularly potent female character, Queen Margaret. She casts a long shadow over the events that occur, and all her vindictive prophecies are proved accurate. Other women have significant roles to play too. The wailing queens, all mothers, represent England and its woes under Richard's tyrannical rule. Ultimately the unfortunate and seemingly powerless Elizabeth triumphs over her enemy by seeing her daughter united with Richmond. Thus it seems that women, who are undoubtedly victims, can also be victors in a male world.

Richard III prepares us for the great tragedies that Shakespeare was to write in the last decade of his life, which focus on the fall of impressive but fatally flawed protagonists: *Othello, Macbeth, King Lear*. Like these celebrated works, *Richard III* is a coherent whole, with a strong and clear direction from the first scene onwards. Shakespeare has abandoned the episodic structure he employed in the *Henry VI* plays in favour of a purposeful and very carefully worked-out structure, in which events and words are mirrored, and **metaphors** and **images** are used to consolidate and expand on the themes he is interested in. This early play also shows us how ingeniously the dramatist used, combined and adapted historical and literary sources to create something original. The rhetoric may be Senecan, but it does not sound false or flat. It has feeling. The **irony** may be More's, but Shakespeare adds his own **puns** and jokes. He breathes life into the history book villain for a wide, non-literary audience to enjoy.

PART TWO

SUMMARIES & COMMENTARIES

Richard III was first published in 1597 in quarto format. It appeared in the Stationers' Register as a **tragedy**. Later, after other quarto reprints, the play was included in the First Folio, a posthumous collection of Shakespeare's plays, which appeared in 1623. At this point it was included in the section of **history plays**. The folio *Richard III* is longer, although some passages which appear in the quarto are not in the folio. Words, phrases and whole passages differ in the two versions, and some characters are left out, or their parts changed, in the folio. We do not know exactly when the play was written, but it seems likely that Shakespeare had finished it by late 1591. It was immensely popular with audiences from the outset (see Stage History).

The text used in the preparation of this Note is the current Arden Shakespeare edition, edited by Antony Hammond (see Further Reading for details).

SYNOPSIS

When the action of *Richard III* opens, Edward IV is king. He has two brothers, George, Duke of Clarence, and Richard, Duke of Gloucester. Together these three men are the most important members of the ruling house of York. The previous king, the Lancastrian Henry VI, was murdered by Gloucester, as was his son Edward, Prince of Wales. Henry's widow, Margaret, survives. She is an important link with the past in this play, and makes a number of prophecies that come true.

Gloucester's villainous nature was first established in *3 Henry VI*, which deals with an earlier period in the Wars of the Roses. Quite early in this drama he announced his intention to 'catch the English crown' (*3 Henry VI*, III.2.179). In *Richard III* he realises this ambition. Richard's egotistical and determined isolation was established in the earlier play too:

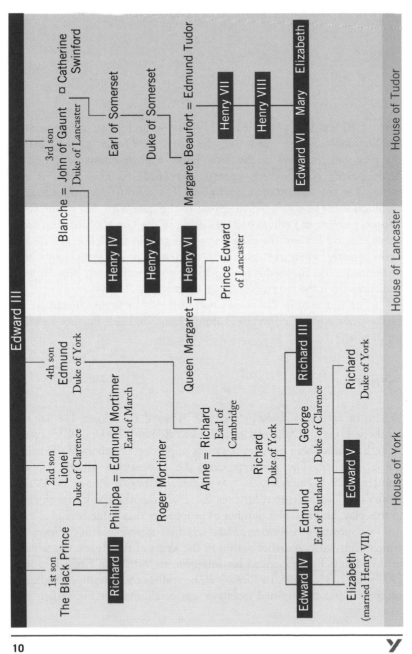

Edward III

1st son — The Black Prince — Richard II

2nd son — Lionel, Duke of Clarence — Philippa = Edmund Mortimer, Earl of March — Roger Mortimer — Anne = Richard, Earl of Cambridge — Richard, Duke of York

4th son — Edmund, Duke of York — Queen Margaret = ...

3rd son — Blanche = John of Gaunt, Duke of Lancaster ☐ Catherine Swinford

Henry IV — Henry V — Henry VI — Prince Edward of Lancaster

Earl of Somerset — Duke of Somerset — Margaret Beaufort = Edmund Tudor — Henry VII — Henry VIII — Edward VI, Mary, Elizabeth

Edward IV — Elizabeth (married Henry VII) — Edmund, Earl of Rutland — Edward V — George, Duke of Clarence — Richard III — Richard, Duke of York

House of York — House of Lancaster — House of Tudor

> I have no brother, I am like no brother;
> And this word 'love', which greybeards call divine,
> Be resident in men like one another,
> And not in me: I am myself alone. (*3 Henry VI*, V.6.80–3)

These words are prophetic. As *Richard III* opens, the villain sets about destroying his brothers in his pursuit for the crown. To begin with, the obstacles look insurmountable. Edward IV and Clarence have heirs who will inherit the throne before Gloucester. But Richard is cunning and energetic. Edward IV is sick and close to death, and Richard is able to contrive the imprisonment and murder of Clarence. He has also set the factions at court at odds, so there is an atmosphere of mistrust. Richard pretends to be friends with everyone while secretly plotting against them. In particular he is working against Edward's wife, Elizabeth, and her kindred. To gain influence Richard marries Anne, the widow of the late Prince of Wales.

Shortly after he hears of Clarence's death, Edward dies. Richard is made Lord Protector because the heir to the throne, Prince Edward, is a minor. Thus he gains more power. He finds an important ally in the Duke of Buckingham. Together these men scheme to have Richard made king. Elizabeth's kindred are imprisoned and put to death, and Prince Edward and his younger brother, the Duke of York, are incarcerated in the Tower of London, where no one is allowed to see them. Justifiably afraid, Richard's mother, the Duchess of York, and Queen Elizabeth have taken sanctuary. Meanwhile Richard sends another ally, Catesby, to sound out Lord Hastings, an important nobleman. He wishes to know if he can count on Hastings's support when he seizes the throne. He cannot, and at a council meeting to discuss the coronation of Edward V, Richard has Hastings arrested as a traitor and put to death.

Gloucester's next move is to have Buckingham address the citizens of London, in order to persuade them that Richard is the only true heir because Edward IV's offspring are illegitimate. The populace remain silent, but Richard eventually achieves the crown when the Lord Mayor and his deputation offer it to him at Baynard's Castle. At first Richard pretends to be reluctant to take on the cares of state, but after much pleading by the wily Buckingham he capitulates and is crowned.

However, Richard does not feel secure. He knows he must dispose of the princes in the Tower if he is to remain on the throne unchallenged. When Buckingham seems hesitant about arranging the murders Richard hires a gentleman, Tyrrel, to do the job. To further strengthen his position Richard decides it is necessary that his wife Anne must die, so that he can marry his niece, Edward and Elizabeth's daughter, Elizabeth.

Meanwhile Buckingham has fled to Wales, where he is gathering an army together. Another invading army, led by Richmond, is set to land in Wales. Richmond has a claim to the throne as a Lancastrian. He gains many supporters, including Stanley, Earl of Derby, who persuades Elizabeth to send her remaining son from her first marriage abroad. Richard sets out to do battle with Buckingham but is intercepted by his mother and Elizabeth, who curse him for his crimes. After a long confrontation Richard appears to gain Elizabeth's consent that he should marry her daughter, although she soon changes her mind and promises the girl to Richmond. Buckingham is captured and executed. Stanley is forced to leave his son with Richard as a hostage. The king is becoming increasingly distrustful as his position grows precarious.

Richmond and Richard clash at Bosworth field in Leicestershire. During the night before the battle the ghosts of Richard's victims appear to the two leaders in their dreams. They curse Richard but predict victory for Richmond. Richard is shaken by his dream, but goes into battle valiantly. Stanley does not come to his support and he faces defeat. When his horse is killed he continues on foot. Eventually he is slain by Richmond, who is immediately offered the crown. Richmond promises to marry Elizabeth's daughter, thus uniting the houses of Lancaster and York and bringing an end to the Wars of the Roses. Peace and prosperity may reign once more.

ACT I

SCENE 1   The civil wars have ended and Richard, Duke of
           Gloucester, finds himself discontented in peacetime. He
           has stirred up trouble between his elder brothers, King
           Edward IV and Clarence. He pretends to be concerned
           when Clarence is imprisoned. He intends to have
           Clarence killed before Edward dies. He also intends to
           marry Lady Anne

The first scene opens with a long **soliloquy** from the protagonist,
who informs us that the country is at peace under his 'glorious' (line 2)
brother Edward's rule. Richard, however, finds peacetime pleasures
uncongenial, partly because he is 'rudely stamp'd' (line 16) and 'not shap'd
for sportive tricks' (line 14). Because he 'cannot prove a lover' (line 28) he
is intent on villainy. To advance himself he has set his elder brothers,
King Edward IV and Clarence, at odds, and he expects to see Clarence
imprisoned shortly 'About a prophecy, which says that "G" / Of Edward's
heirs the murderer shall be' (lines 39–40). Clarence is brought in under
armed guard on his way to the Tower of London, where he is to be held.
Richard expresses sympathy for his brother, blaming Queen Elizabeth
and her family for Clarence's arrest. He promises to intercede with
Edward to get Clarence released. When his brother is led away by
Brakenbury, Lord Hastings enters. He has just been released from the
Tower. He tells Richard that Edward is 'sickly, weak and melancholy'
(line 136), and that his doctors fear for his life. When Hastings
leaves, Richard remains onstage to outline his plans to have Clarence
killed before Edward dies. He is also determined to marry the Earl of
Warwick's daughter, Anne, who was formerly married to Prince Edward,
the deposed Henry VI's son.

> Richard's first soliloquy is unusual and compelling. Shakespeare's
> villains rarely introduce themselves to us so directly and
> purposefully this early in the proceedings. By opening the play with
> Richard, Shakespeare gives the protagonist's view of his world
> pre-eminence and enables his magnificent villain to draw the
> audience in. Are we being encouraged to collude with Gloucester at
> the start of the play? This soliloquy also functions as a kind of

prologue, with Richard acting the role of chorus (a figure who would not normally participate in the action of the play). Thus we are immediately aware of the protagonist as an actor. This idea is a very central one in the play. We also immediately sense that everything that will occur in this drama depends upon Richard; the play has a central figure as its focus right from the start.

To begin with, Richard speaks in general terms, comparing and contrasting the recent wars with peacetime, which he characterises as 'weak' (line 24). Descriptions of the civil war always precede remarks about peace, suggesting that Richard prefers the battlefield to ladies' chambers and lutes, which he has little time or respect for. Even before he has declared his own villainy, we sense that the protagonist is a man of action who enjoys dissent and combat. In particular, Richard's **personification** of War, converted into a narcissistic, capering lover, suggests the protagonist's antipathy to peacetime pleasures (see lines 9–13). We might also feel that his caustic and scornful remarks about amorous behaviour at court are misogynistic. Throughout this scene Richard is antagonistic towards women and their influence on men. This antipathy will remain a feature of his characterisation, although, as we shall see, he can be devastatingly effective when he chooses to act the role of wooer.

Richard's general discontent is explained when he starts to describe himself and his own 'deformity' at line 16. Is Shakespeare offering us a reason for Richard's villainy? At this point we begin to see what might be characterised as Richard's egotism: the word 'I' is stressed a number of times in the rest of the soliloquy. But narcissistic Richard is no self-deluding fool. He sees himself clearly. He coolly acknowledges that he lacks the physical beauty necessary to prosper as a lover at court. Richard's physical appearance sounds alarming and repellent: 'Cheated of feature by dissembling Nature, / Deform'd, unfinish'd, sent before my time / Into this breathing world scarce half made up', 'curtail'd' (lines 18–21). This is entirely appropriate for a villain. The Elizabethan audience would have recognised that the protagonist's deformed exterior reflected inner viciousness. As the play progresses, Richard's hideous deformities –

of body and mind – are elaborated on as he is cursed by the female characters: his mother, Margaret, Elizabeth and his hapless wife Anne. We will be reminded many times of the protagonist's loathsome attributes, which become firm proof of his monstrous wickedness.

But what is Richard's attitude to his ugliness? He accepts it. Perhaps there is even **ironic** enjoyment of it in lines 14–27. The amusing description of dogs barking at him in the streets shows his sangfroid, befitting a man who will revel in his own evil. Instead of hurrying past to avoid the curs that draw attention to his physical faults, he tells us, 'I halt by them' (line 23). Three lines later Richard describes his shadow, in a line that recalls the image of Edward as this 'glorious ... son [sun] of York'. Even before he tells us that he is a villain, we know that Richard of Gloucester is intent on causing trouble in the realm; his dark presence will cast a long shadow over England until he is defeated by Richmond. The very negative terms Richard employs when describing himself point to two things: his isolation and 'difference'.

Because he 'cannot prove a lover' (line 28), Richard tells us that he is 'determined to prove a villain' (line 30). His words are bold and firm. He insists on the negative, as he has done throughout this opening speech. We see Richard's characteristic enjoyment of wordplay and double meanings. The protagonist's wickedness is 'determined' in two ways: firstly, through strength of will and cunning he will achieve his ends; secondly, because he is deformed, it is Richard's destiny to be a villain. Richard was born bad but, significantly, he also chooses wickedness. His brazen attitude is powerfully compelling and, at this stage, appealing. Richard seems to be enjoying himself immensely when he outlines the plots he has laid which will prove how 'subtle, false, and treacherous' (line 37) he is. As proof of the efficacy of his villainy, Clarence appears '*with a guard of Men*' immediately after Richard describes how he has ensnared his brother.

We will continue to marvel at Richard during the exchanges that follow because we see how adept he is at assuming roles. Thus we are introduced to a theme common in Elizabethan drama: the difficulty of negotiating appearances and reality (see Themes). There is a good deal of pleasure to be had in watching a successful actor at work. We will also enjoy the irony of Gloucester's dealings with others here – another feature of the play that is established early. Richard plays the loving, faithful, teary-eyed brother with Clarence and sympathises with Hastings. He also pretends to be worried by the news of Edward's poor health, suggesting not simply his family loyalty, but also his concern for the state of the nation. In his conversations with both Clarence and Hastings, Richard disparages Queen Elizabeth and her relatives, blaming them for the ills that have befallen the two noblemen. Richard is already manipulating others for his own ends. He wants to encourage further dissent at court; he also intends his brother and Hastings to believe that he supports them: '*we* are not safe!' (line 70, my emphasis) he exclaims to Clarence. By suggesting that he too is threatened, he convinces his brother of his loyalty and innocence. Throughout his conversations with Clarence and Hastings, Richard flatters his victims, telling them what they want to hear. This is a technique he will make use of many times in his dealings with the other characters in this play. You will notice that the dialogue is less formal in these exchanges; Richard is a master of different speech styles.

Unlike Clarence and Hastings, we are not taken in by his false bonhomie and brotherliness. Richard's brutality is confirmed by the decisive speeches he makes when he is alone at lines 117 and 145. The swift changes in tone are chilling; Richard's assurances are bold and blunt: 'Go, tread the path that thou shalt ne'er return' (line 117); 'He cannot live, I hope, and must not die / Till George be pack'd with post-horse up to Heaven' (lines 145–6). The force of these lines is intensified when Richard says he will 'bustle' in the world (line 152). The verb expresses his energy perfectly.

Richard does not reveal all his motives in this opening scene. Like the medieval Vice, he is simply a personification of evil; Shakespeare is not concerned to explore the villain's motivation in great depth. There is enough mystery, however, to keep us enthralled, in spite of the fact that we know what the outcome of the play will be. Richard teases the audience at lines 157–8 with hints about 'another secret close intent'. At the end of Act I Scene 1 we are eager to see how Gloucester manages to succeed in his aims. In particular we are intrigued by the idea of Richard as wooer – especially since he has expressed such scorn for eager lovers in this opening scene. In spite of his deformities, he seems confident that he will be able to make a match of it with Lady Anne, whose husband and father he killed. How can he expect to seduce a woman who must hate him? Shakespeare is preparing us for the fascinating confrontation that occurs in the next scene. Richard's casual and insouciant confession of murder is both alarming and thrilling, confirmation that we are watching a very dangerous man at work. But we cannot help but be drawn in when he addresses us directly with a question at line 154. Like his victims, we are, at this point, unable to resist Richard's evil charm.

The scene ends on a practical note as Gloucester summarises the obstacles he must overcome if he is to thrive. With the confidence and skill he has shown in the first 160 lines of the play, we know he will achieve his diabolical aims. Our pleasure will come in seeing *how* he achieves them.

2 **this son of York** Richard is **punning** on son/sun. Edward IV chose the sun as his emblem after he had a vision of three suns, which appeared to him before a battle that took place during the Wars of the Roses (*3 Henry VI*, II.1.25–40). His father, Richard, Duke of York, was killed in 1460

27 **descant** a musical term; a singer sings a melody against a fixed harmony. Richard is using the word to mean comment

45 **the Tower** the Tower of London, which served as a prison as well as a royal residence. High-born prisoners were kept in the Tower

55 **cross-row** alphabet

64 **Lady Grey** Elizabeth Woodeville was first married to Sir John Grey. Her subsequent marriage to Edward IV was not a popular match with the nobility of England, firstly because of her inferior rank, but also because Edward advanced a number of her relatives. Richard makes much of this when he insults Queen Elizabeth's family in Act I Scene 3

67 **Anthony Woodeville** Earl Rivers, Elizabeth's brother

73 **Mistress Shore** Elizabeth Shore, also called Jane Shore. She was the
mistress of both Edward IV and Hastings. Richard profits from her
scandalous reputation when he makes his move against Hastings in Act III

77 **my Lord Chamberlain** Hastings

115 **lie for you** Richard is indulging in wordplay at his brother's expense. He
leads Clarence to believe that he is prepared to sacrifice himself for his
cause, i.e. to risk imprisonment on his behalf. The audience will pick up on
the other, more sinister meaning: that Richard is ready and willing to tell
lies in order to achieve his own ends

153 **Warwick's youngest daughter** Anne Neville, who was the widow of
Henry VI's son, Edward, Prince of Wales. Her father, the Earl of Warwick,
was known as the 'kingmaker' because of the great power and influence
he had

160 **run before my horse to market** a proverbial expression, typical of Richard.
Here he suggests that he should not attempt to run before he can walk, i.e.
that he needs to deal with one scheme at a time and not get ahead of
himself

SCENE 2   **Lady Anne follows the corpse of Henry VI as a mourner.
She also bewails the fate of her late husband, Henry's son.
Richard woos Anne**

Henry VI's body is being taken for burial. Lady Anne accompanies the
'hearse' (line 2). She is in mourning for her husband, Edward, as well as
his father, Henry VI. She curses Richard, who was responsible for both
deaths. When Gloucester enters she castigates him as an inhuman,
unnatural and devilish butcher. Richard defends himself, saying that he
committed the murders because he loves Anne and wishes to marry her.
Initially Anne is scornful of – and repulsed by – Richard. She spits on
him. But as he continues to woo her she finds it impossible to resist him.
When Richard offers her his sword so that she might revenge Henry's
and Edward's deaths by killing him, Anne finds that she cannot be his
'executioner' (line 189). Richard asks her to wear his ring, swearing that
he is Anne's 'poor devoted servant' (line 210) and says that he will visit
her after he has seen Henry buried and has 'wet his grave with my
repentant tears' (line 219). Anne is glad to observe his penitence and
leaves the stage feeling well disposed towards her skilful wooer. Richard

is exultant. He revels in his brilliance as a lover and **ironically** suggests that perhaps he is 'a marvellous proper man' after all (line 259).

> In this scene Richard's ability to dominate others is confirmed. In Act I Scene 1 we saw him gulling his brother and Hastings so that they believed he had their best interests at heart. Here the obstacle he has to overcome – Anne's hatred – seems to be a much tougher proposition. C.W.R.D. Moseley has described the wooing of Anne as 'a farcical grotesque' (*Richard III*, Penguin Critical Studies, 1989, p. 62). To begin with, Richard's task seems impossible. Anne's opening lamentations have been characterised as histrionic. Her curses against Richard are full of venom; **images** of devils, bloody death and extreme misery dominate. Is Anne, as some critics suggest, revelling in her victimisation? Even if she is, we are uncomfortable when she curses Richard's future wife: we know that she is cursing herself. The irony here is cruel. However we feel about Anne as mourner, it is entirely appropriate that Henry VI's death is dwelt on at length, reminding us of the bloody history of the Wars of the Roses, which destroyed the houses of Lancaster and York. On many occasions in *Richard III*, characters refer to the events of the past and make prophecies about the future; thus Shakespeare encourages his audience to view Richard's role in history as providential. The villain is God's scourge, his reign the dire consequence of his ancestors' and enemies' crimes. Throughout the play curses will link the past, present and future, as Anne's do in this scene.

Anne is no less venomous when Richard enters. From line 34 to line 188 she vents her fury and loathing with violent and scornful words. Her contempt is conveyed by her use of the pronouns 'thou' and 'thy', while her wooer adopts the more polite forms 'you' and 'your'. Anne is vengeful, telling Richard that he should hang himself. But when she is offered the opportunity of revenge, she cannot take it. What happens to her? She is gradually taken in. Like a spider which spins a web to catch a fly, Richard craftily ensnares her with words. He always has an answer for her, and he flatters her. He brazenly tells her that he is fit for her bedchamber, and that her beauty led him to commit murder. Richard takes control of the conversation, focusing on his 'love' (note how he plays with this word) and her loveliness. By line 155, when Richard makes a long speech in which he describes how Anne's scornful looks have 'drawn salt tears' (line 157) from his eyes, we know his victim is lost. The final lines of this speech, when Richard bares his breast and offers Anne his sword, confirm his extraordinary, perverse – even mystical – power. We are transfixed as he invokes his crimes as proof of his love. His dogged determination to win Anne has been characterised by dark irony of this kind.

Anne drops the sword and capitulates. She knows she should not be taken in – she calls Richard a 'dissembler' (line 188) – but she is. She allows herself to accept the protestations of affection she hears as truth. Perhaps she is even colluding with her seducer. The verse form at lines 196–206 hints at this. Here the dialogue continues in **stichomythia** which resembles a love song; Richard insists on his devotion and Anne coyly agrees to accept his ring. This is a symbol of their betrothal – the couple are now committed to one another. In *A Commentary on Shakespeare's Richard III* (1968), W.H. Clemen reminds us of the Elizabethan proverb 'To give a thing and take a thing is to wear the devil's gold ring' (p. 36). Do we pity Anne, or is it impossible to sympathise with her because she has allowed herself to be won over so swiftly by false words? Has she made a pact with the devil? Perhaps, but we recognise that Richard has appealed to her best instincts; he has convinced her that she should forgive, even if she cannot forget. He has also, of course, feigned penitence.

In the final **soliloquy** Richard reverts to the playful and dismissive tone we heard when he was alone in Act I Scene 1. With rhetorical questions he draws us in again, reminding us of the obstacles he faced. The structure of this scene is similar to the opening scene: both begin and end with soliloquies. Here we are forced to agree that it is indeed miraculous that Richard has won Anne's heart. We may even feel inclined to share some of Richard's contempt for his 'love' when we hear about the late Prince Edward's virtues. How could Anne debase herself so? Richard seems justified in revelling in his own villainy and deformity. The last lines of the scene recall the reference he made to himself as a shadow in the previous scene, reminding us that Richard is focused on himself. His victims do not hold the same fascination for him. We know this because he does not waste many words on Anne, telling us simply and brutally that he 'will not keep her long' (line 234).

s.d. **Halberds** a halberd was a weapon, made up of a spear and battleaxe

4 **virtuous Lancaster** Henry VI was known for his piety

29 **Chertsey** a famous abbey on the Thames, about twenty miles outside London

30 **Paul's** St Paul's Cathedral

55–6 **dead Henry's wounds ... afresh** according to folklore, a dead person's wounds would begin to bleed again when the murderer was present

96 **falchion** sword

154 **basilisks** mythical creatures which could kill with a glance

161 **Rutland** the second eldest son of Richard, Duke of York, and brother to Edward IV, Clarence and Gloucester. He was killed by the Lancastrians during the Wars of the Roses

163 **thy warlike father** Richard Neville, Earl of Warwick, who was defeated by Edward IV and killed in battle in 1471

164 **my father's death** Richard, Duke of York, was captured and put to death after the Battle of Wakefield in 1460

204 **All men, I hope, live so** a traditional Christian belief that man should live in hope of salvation through Christ's suffering. Anne's words draw attention to Richard's evil. Throughout the play he mocks the tenets and ceremonies of organised religion

206 **To take is not to give** Anne appears to be 'hedging her bets' here, but in spite of her reluctance to commit herself, her words show that she has accepted the ring, and, therefore, Richard

216 **Crosby Place** also referred to as Crosby House. It was one of Richard's London residences, situated on Bishopsgate Street

231 **Whitefriars** a Carmelite priory on Fleet Street in London. Shakespeare seems to make an error here. Henry's body was actually taken to Blackfriars, which was on the Thames

246 **Tewkesbury** Henry VI's son, Prince Edward, was killed in 1471 at Tewkesbury. Shakespeare dramatises his death in *3 Henry VI*, with Edward IV, Clarence and Gloucester all taking turns to stab the young prince

256 **denier** a small sum of money. Richard makes a much greater wager at the
end of the play when he calls for a horse on Bosworth field. It is apt that
Richard should appear to be a betting man: in the opening speech he
aligned himself with the devil and denied God and his conscience when he
said he was 'determined to prove a villain'. He is gambling with his
immortal soul

259 **proper** handsome and attractive

SCENE 3   Edward's wife, Queen Elizabeth, is concerned about her
husband's failing health. Buckingham announces that
Edward IV wishes to reconcile the warring factions at
court, but Richard continues to stir up trouble with
Queen Elizabeth's relations. Queen Margaret curses the
assembled company. Richard arranges the murder of
Clarence

Elizabeth's brother, Lord Rivers, and her son by her first marriage,
Lord Grey, attempt to comfort the queen, but she is concerned about the
fate of her family should Edward die. Richard is to be established as
Protector, and she knows that he is her enemy. Buckingham and Stanley
have been visiting Edward, who is in good spirits in spite of his
poor health. He intends to 'make atonement / Between the Duke of
Gloucester' and Queen Elizabeth's brothers and 'between them and
my Lord Chamberlain' (lines 36–8). Elizabeth's heart remains heavy;
she cannot bring herself to believe that a reconciliation is really possible.

Richard bursts in, complaining that he has been misrepresented by
the 'lewd complaints' (line 61) of the queen. He is bitter about the
advancement of her relations. He accuses Elizabeth of having Clarence
and Hastings imprisoned and insults her. While Elizabeth and Richard
quarrel, Queen Margaret enters. She reminds us of Richard's crimes,
interrupting the altercation to denounce the assembled company for
deposing her husband, Henry VI. They respond with accusations of their
own (Margaret was responsible for the death of Richard's brother
Rutland). Margaret is not deterred from her purpose. She curses each of
the characters in turn and prophesies their destruction. She warns the
company against Richard. When she leaves, Buckingham and Rivers
seem shaken. By way of contrast, Richard is calm. Hypocritically he says

he repents the wrongs he has done Margaret. He then returns to the inflammatory topic of Clarence. Just as the squabbling resumes, Catesby arrives. Edward wishes to see Elizabeth and the courtiers. Alone onstage Richard is well satisfied with the trouble he has caused. He dispatches two murderers to the Tower, warning them not to listen to Clarence's pleadings.

Richard continues to dominate and control others in this scene, dealing confidently with the accusations levelled against him. His habit of interrupting others helps him gain control and confirms his toughness. For much of the scene Richard plays the discontented innocent, grumbling that it is impossible to be 'a plain man' who thinks 'no harm' (line 51) because 'the world is grown so bad' (line 70). But Richard is more subtle and sophisticated than this; his feigned anger enables him to insult the other characters while pretending that he wishes to be friends with them. In this way he is able to keep the feud at court going. Elizabeth seems to take some of Richard's remarks at face value, although she clearly – and wisely – distrusts her brother-in-law, as her speech at line 74 suggests: 'Come, come: we know your meaning, brother Gloucester.'

Our enjoyment of Richard's hypocritical posturing is heightened when Margaret enters. While he is busy acting out his latest role, she reminds us of the villain's true character in her vengeful **asides**. Thus Shakespeare provides two views of the protagonist simultaneously, adding to his theatrical power and the impression of evil that is being created. We can never forget how dangerous and treacherous Gloucester is. Margaret dominates the scene from the moment she appears. She is impossible to ignore, even before she is acknowledged when she steps forward. She resembles a Greek Fury, while also taking on some of the functions of the **chorus**, whose role is to comment on the action. Her invective is powerful and eloquent; **ironically**, like her enemy Richard, she retains her wits when she is attacked. Her vengeful utterances make Margaret a compelling figure, and we recognise the wisdom of her warnings against the 'bottled spider' Richard (line 242). However, it is difficult to feel much sympathy for the former queen. She is too vindictive, too full of vitriolic hatred – and she is not guiltless, as Elizabeth's family all remind her.

We gradually come to respect Margaret's judgement. She links the past, present and future through her invective, reminding us of the cycle of guilt and expiation that has characterised the Wars of the Roses. All of her prophecies come true, and she is one of the few characters who is able to stand up to Richard effectively. Her confrontation with him is compelling. Richard attacks the old woman as viciously as she speaks to him, but it takes him some time to bring her up short. When he breaks into one of her vituperative speeches at line 233 the former queen is put off balance momentarily, recovering to make further aspersions and warnings before she takes her leave. Neither Richard's joke, Dorset's derision, nor Buckingham's pleas can prevent Margaret from speaking her mind.

When the former queen departs, Richard swiftly takes charge of the conversation again, and the quarrel resumes. We can enjoy another moment of comedy when he makes his aside at line 318. It will come as a relief after Margaret's outpourings. Shakespeare uses Richard's final **soliloquy** to keep us informed about the progress of the villain's plots and explain his motivation: Gloucester seeks to destroy Elizabeth's relatives as well as his own brother. Richard's use of 'Holy Writ' (line 337) is clearly intended to show the depths to which this devil will sink. Richard's character becomes blacker in each successive scene. Richard's reference to scripture also prepares us for his abuse of religion later on. In Act III Scene 7 he will be discovered with a prayer book in his hand, flanked by two bishops. It comes as no surprise that Richard deals with his brother's murderers swiftly and coolly. The colloquial language he employs from line 340 to the end of the scene is further proof of his decisive energy. When Richard tells us that he plays the devil we are reminded of the theme of appearance and reality (see Themes).

It is difficult to feel much sympathy for the 'wrangling pirates' (line 158) we see in this scene, even though we recognise that they are being manipulated by Richard (with the exception of Margaret, who does not really participate in the action of the play). This is because the characters are all selfish and self-righteous. As yet it is difficult to read Buckingham's character, although his cool diplomacy hints that he is a political animal we must watch closely.

s.d. **Grey ... Dorset** Queen Elizabeth's sons from her first marriage

14 **Protector** the Protector was in charge of the realm during the minority of the king; he was the most powerful individual in the kingdom

20 **Countess Richmond** Margaret Beaufort, whose first husband was Edmund Tudor. Stanley, Earl of Derby, was her third husband. Richmond, the Lancastrian claimant to the throne who defeats Richard III at the end of the play, was her son by Edmund Tudor

s.d. **Queen Margaret** Margaret of Anjou was the widow of Henry VI. Her appearance in the play is not based on historical fact. She returned to France in 1476, dying in 1482 before Richard became king

130 **Saint Albans** Queen Elizabeth's first husband, Sir John Grey, was killed at the Battle of St Albans in 1461. Richard seems to be implying that Margaret was responsible for this battle

135 **his father Warwick** Clarence married Warwick's elder daughter, Isabel, in 1469. Clarence helped his father-in-law restore Henry VI to the throne in 1470, treacherously working against his brother Edward, who was king at the time. Later he changed allegiances and returned to the Yorkist cause, helping Edward to defeat Warwick

144 **cacodemon** an evil spirit; one of many references linking Richard to the devil

228 **elvish-mark'd, abortive** the implication is that Richard was destined for evil from birth, when fairies put their mark on him. His premature ('abortive') birth is another sinister sign

255 **malapert** impudent

353 **eyes drop millstones** a proverbial expression that is used here to imply hard-heartedness

SCENE 4   Clarence is murdered

Incarcerated in the Tower, Clarence recounts a terrible dream he has had to his keeper. He dreamt that he was sailing to Burgundy with his brother Richard, who stumbled on deck and pushed Clarence overboard. Clarence paints a terrifying picture of 'the slimy bottom of the deep' (line 32) and the 'tempest to my soul' (line 44) that occurred while he was drowning. He asks the keeper to sit by him awhile because he is frightened and wishes to sleep. Brakenbury, Lieutenant of the Tower, enters, shortly followed by the two murderers, who announce that Clarence must be delivered into their hands. Brakenbury seems to fear the worst, but resigns his charge.

The second murderer is unsure of himself. He fears damnation. His lack of certainty affects his companion, whose conscience is awakened. By this point the second murderer has found his courage, claiming that conscience makes men cowards. The two men decide to drag Clarence into the next room and drown him in a butt of malmsey. Their victim wakes up. The murderers hesitate but Clarence guesses why they have come. He urges them not to kill him because it is unlawful, and because murder is a sin. The murderers remind Clarence of the crimes he committed during the Wars of the Roses. When Clarence tells them to go to his brother Richard, who, he says, will reward them for saving his life, the murderers tell him the truth: it was not Edward but Gloucester who sent them to destroy him. Again Clarence urges the murderers to 'Relent, and save your souls' (line 246), but it is too late. He is stabbed and dragged out by the first murderer. The second murderer is full of remorse; the first knows that he will not be safe when Clarence's death is discovered. When he has buried the corpse and collected his reward, he will flee.

A key theme in the play is established in this scene: conscience. Throughout Act I Scene 4 the characters are concerned with guilt, damnation, repentance and remorse. Clarence's dream **foreshadows** Richard's at Bosworth field, although Richard's nightmare is conveyed in a style that is very different from the subtle poetry of this scene. Unlike his villainous brother, Clarence acknowledges the importance of his immortal soul and makes the correct moral choices before he dies. He confesses his sins. His terrible vision leads him to repent. But is it too late? Surely this scene suggests that Clarence, in spite of his remorse, is destined for eternal torment?

Clarence's dream recalls the ancient Roman writer Seneca, especially in its depiction of a watery hell. The pain of drowning, the sinister character of the sea and the 'foul fiends' (line 58) who encircle

Clarence are vividly evoked. Water was frequently a symbol of death in ancient mythology. Shakespeare appeals to all the senses in lines 21–63 as he describes the sights and sounds that Clarence suffers during the 'tempest' that racks his soul. We are offered a clear picture of the terrors of hell – no wonder the doomed man is horribly afraid. It is to his credit that Clarence repents his crimes, but the past catches up with him here, just as it will catch up with Richard on Bosworth field in Act V. Clarence seems to acknowledge that it is just that he is punished for his part in the Wars of the Roses. 'But Thou wilt be aveng'd on my misdeeds' (line 70) he says, hoping that God will not also avenge Himself on the rest of his family. Clarence's guilt is important for a number of reasons. Firstly, it links him to the rest of the 'wrangling pirates' we saw in the previous scene; like them he is tainted, and like them he must suffer, as Margaret predicted. Secondly, this scene suggests that Shakespeare is concerned to dramatise Richard's reign as a moral lesson. Gloucester is the unwitting scourge of God; by murdering his guilty kindred he is cleansing the realm. We must see the justice of this. The seriousness of the dramatist's purpose is conveyed by Clarence's dignified rhetoric, which is completely different in tone from everything we have heard so far in this play. The rich but ominous **imagery** of Clarence's speeches lends the speaker pathos and gravity. Thirdly, we see here the dreadful consequences of making bad moral choices. We know that Richard, whose crimes – ultimately – will be far more heinous than his brother's, will suffer horribly when he dies.

Shakespeare drives this point home firmly by showing the murderers' moral uncertainty. Each in turn is afflicted by his conscience. Their hesitation at line 163 increases their victim's dignity and heightens the dramatic tension of the scene, while also demonstrating the enormity of the crime which will be committed. The way in which the murderers debate with each other, and then with Clarence, recalls Richard's persuasive techniques of the previous scenes in Act I. We are being reminded where all the altercations in this play lead: to physical and moral death. What are we to make of the second murderer's reference to Pilate? Are

we supposed to see Clarence as an innocent Christ-like figure?
Perhaps not. The religious reference is another reminder of the
consequences of making bad moral choices. It is fitting that it is
the second murderer, who urged his companion to 'Take the devil
in thy mind' (line 141), who now recalls the blood on Pilate's hands:
he sees what he has done, like his victim before his death. We, of
course, also see that the devil who pushed these two murderers to
commit the crime is Richard. Even when he is not present we are
aware of the villain as stage manager. The murderers seem to be
infected by Richard's diabolical humour, as the black jokes they
make suggest. The **irony** of the scene is also Ricardian, especially
the timing and manner of Clarence's death. Immediately before this
we wince as we watch the scales fall from Clarence's eyes when he
realises the extent of his brother's treachery. Like all Richard's other
victims in the play, this one is confronted by his own faulty
judgement before he dies. Margaret warned everyone to be wary of
Richard, but the morally frail victims realise their folly too late. By
the end of the scene each character has his just rewards for his
crimes. Clarence has been forced to pay for his sins, while the two
murderers will be haunted until they die. The tense and urgent last
lines of the scene make this palpably clear.

10 **Burgundy** Clarence's sister Margaret was married to the Duke of Burgundy,
which was a large duchy at this time, incorporating the Netherlands

45–6 **melancholy flood … ferryman** a reference to Greek mythology. In order to
reach the land of the dead, dead souls would be ferried across the River
Styx by Charon

50 **perjury** a reference to Clarence's double dealings during the Wars of the
Roses. He returned to his brother Edward's cause in 1471, having sworn
allegiance to Warwick and Henry VI

101 **Judgement Day** according to Christian belief, on the day when the world
ends, the dead will rise and God will judge all men and women

147 **malmsey-butt** a barrel of wine. Malmsey was a wine from Greece

184 **King of kings** God. Edward will refer to Him too in Act II Scene 1, at line
13, ironically echoing his dead brother's words

185 **table of His law** the Ten Commandments. The sixth commandment, which is
pertinent here, is 'Thou shalt not kill'

231 **as snow in harvest** proverbial. The implication is that Richard is frozen and cruel

248 **beastly, savage, devilish** Clarence's words remind us of Richard's inhumanity, and the fact that he is damned. Throughout the play the women curse the villain as a savage and diabolical animal, while Richard mocks those who are afflicted by their consciences

262 **Pilate** Pontius Pilate was the Roman governor of Judaea at the time when Jesus was crucified. After the Crucifixion he washed his hands publicly and declared that he was not responsible for Jesus's death and had only allowed it to occur because he had been pressurised by the Jews

ACT II

SCENE 1   **The warring factions make peace at court. Edward is disturbed to learn of Clarence's death**

The ailing Edward believes that he has reconciled the warring factions at court. Hastings and Rivers, Dorset and Buckingham, profess their loyalty to one another. When Richard enters Edward cheerfully proclaims the success of the 'deeds of charity' (line 50) that have been performed. Gloucester appears to fall in with the happy mood, saying that it is 'death to me to be at enmity' with anyone (line 61). However, when Elizabeth asks Edward to be reconciled to Clarence, his tone changes and he pretends to be insulted. The company is shocked when Richard demands, 'Who knows not that the gentle Duke is dead?' (line 80). This dramatic revelation has a profound effect on Edward. When Stanley enters to ask Edward's pardon for one of his servants who has killed a gentleman in a brawl, Edward reproaches the others, asking why no one begged him to spare Clarence. He is full of grief, remembering his brother's services to him during the Wars of the Roses. Like the dead Clarence, Edward fears that God's 'justice will take hold / On me, and you, and mine and yours for this' (lines 132–3). As the king is helped from the stage, Richard takes the opportunity to blame Elizabeth's kindred for Clarence's death.

This is an uneasy scene of hypocrisy and professed remorse, which builds on the themes established in the previous scene. We doubt the sincerity of the lords who profess to love one another, in spite of Edward's assurance. Thus the very first ceremony we see enacted in the play is flawed. Hereafter we know not to trust any of the rituals that Richard is involved in. We might also feel uncomfortable listening to Edward's speech of reproach at line 103. Although he says that he reversed the order for his brother's death, he must surely accept some of the blame for what has happened. The Elizabethan audience, aware of the historical truth, would have known that Clarence's fault was great. He plotted to overthrow Edward: an act of treason that attracted the death penalty. Thus Edward's words 'My brother kill'd no man: his fault was thought' (line 105) ring false. Like Clarence, Edward realises the truth too late. It seems that the brothers share the same faulty judgement: neither recognises Richard's treachery. This is **ironic**, as is the fact that Clarence's death is shown to lead directly to Edward's. We know that he will die soon when he is helped from the stage at the end of the scene. Stanley's plea provides another example of painful irony. Given the roles that both Clarence and Edward played in the Wars of the Roses, the audience might recognise that it is just that neither finds peace before he dies.

Meanwhile, we see that the supreme ironist, Richard, has firmly maintained his control by indirect means. At the end of Act I we knew his first plot had a successful outcome. This is confirmed publicly in this scene. The confident hypocrisy he displays here is already familiar from Act I Scene 3. We are aware that his words have a snide and insinuating edge, especially in his speech at line 53. The fluidity of the lines reveals how capable Richard is of dissembling. His final devastatingly insincere remark, 'I thank God for my humility' (line 73), will surely raise a laugh from the audience. Richard's power is confirmed when we see him interpret others' looks at the end of the scene in his final speech. Is it significant that it is Buckingham who answers him here? Does this suggest that the enigmatic politician is drawing closer to the **Machiavellian** villain?

89 **Mercury** the Roman messenger of the gods, renowned for his speed. In mythology he is depicted wearing winged sandals

90 **Some tardy cripple** a black and ironic joke at Richard's own expense; he was responsible for the 'countermand' himself, as we know

105 **his fault was thought** a proverbial expression. By suggesting that Clarence was guilty of nothing worse than thought, Edward seems to be downplaying his treason. Shakespeare is concerned to show Clarence's virtue and innocence in order to make Richard's fratricide even more heinous

124 **The precious image of our dear Redeemer** during the Renaissance, theological images were highly valued. According to scripture, God created man in His own image

134 **closet** private chamber

SCENE 2 **The Duchess of York and Elizabeth mourn Edward's death. His son Edward, Prince of Wales, is to be brought to London to be crowned**

Clarence's children try to discover the truth about their father's death. Ironically they believe that Edward is to blame, having been told by their 'good uncle Gloucester' (line 20) that he was 'provok'd' (line 21) by Elizabeth. The Duchess of York expresses her shame as Richard's mother. She is interrupted by the arrival of Elizabeth, who is deeply distressed because Edward has died. The women and children join in lamentation. Rivers advises Elizabeth to send for Prince Edward, so that he can be crowned swiftly. When he enters Richard pretends to be in mourning for his brother and sympathises with his sister-in-law. Buckingham begins to take an active role in the affairs of state, proposing that 'some little train' (line 120) should be sent to accompany Prince Edward from Ludlow to London. Rivers is immediately suspicious, but Buckingham says that a small party is necessary to avoid new trouble in the realm. A meeting is to be held to determine who should go to Ludlow. When he is alone with Richard it becomes clear that Buckingham is in Richard's confidence, and that the two are plotting to 'part the Queen's proud kindred from the Prince' (line 150). Richard flatters his accomplice, saying that he will be guided by his counsel.

> Up to Richard's entrance the scene focuses on the way in which the characters onstage react to the deaths of Edward and Clarence. The plot is not being developed; the action only moves forward again with Gloucester's arrival. The static lamentation scene is

nonetheless important. The children's desire to learn the truth
about their father's end continues the theme of guilt, linking Act II
Scene 2 to the two scenes that precede it. Their innocent trust in
Richard makes us uncomfortable, **foreshadowing** the alarm that
will be felt when we watch the wicked uncle persuade the young
princes to lodge in the Tower in the next scene. Here Richard's
ability to dupe and manipulate children with false shows of
affection adds to the impression of the villain's depravity. He shows
as little mercy for women and children as he shows for his fellow
men. The children's piety reinforces an important point about God
as the only true revenger, and it is appropriate that Richard is
referred to immediately after the children have offered to pray:
again Shakespeare is reminding us of Richard as unwitting scourge.
Even when he is not present, Richard continues to cast a shadow
over everything. The Duchess of York's reiterated story of the
family deaths that have occurred during the recent wars reminds us
of the historical context, extending our understanding of the cycle
of crime and punishment. The mother's shame and her astute
description of her youngest surviving son as the 'one false glass'
(line 53) she has left are as poignant as her tears and breast-beating.
The lamentation scenes in *Richard III* may seem artificial and
exaggerated to modern audiences, but we cannot deny the power of
the grief that is expressed.

The poignancy of the scene increases with Elizabeth's agonised
arrival. To begin with, the women compete with one another, each
claiming to have the greatest reason for sorrow. This kind of
competitiveness was commonplace in lamentation scenes in
Classical drama and academic disputations. But Shakespeare's use
of **antanaclasis** at lines 74–9 shows that all the characters onstage
gradually come to speak in harmony as they express their shared
feelings of woe. The rhetorical devices used in this scene add to the
solemnity of the mourning. While the women and children seem
paralysed by grief, Rivers and Dorset seek to temper their sorrow
and remind them of the present and future: young Prince Edward.
However, Richard enters at this point, and we know that it is
already too late for Edward IV's vulnerable heir. Again Gloucester's

arrival forces a change in tone. He mocks his mother, and then Buckingham makes an empty and calculated speech of platitudes intended to comfort Elizabeth. He speaks smoothly, ingeniously introducing a new plan that immediately makes Rivers suspicious. But he is as much a master wordsmith as Richard; he very quickly rebuffs objections and the women are hoodwinked. Rivers seems to remain uneasy, signified by his use of 'I think' at line 134, but he too falls in with the plans presented to him. By the end of the scene we already have proof that Buckingham and Richard are an effective combined force. The urgency of Buckingham's last speech contrasts with the solemn, symmetrical and more leisurely phrasing used by the women and children earlier. The pair are ready to strike. However, we realise that Buckingham is a fool to align himself with the villain when we hear Gloucester's false and flattering last lines. Is Buckingham as much a dupe as Anne was in Act I? It seems ironic that this scene opens and closes with children, the innocence of Clarence's grieving offspring obliterated by Richard's cunning reference to himself as 'a child' who will be directed by his 'dear cousin' (lines 152–3) Buckingham.

s.d. **Duchess of York** Richard's mother, the widow of Richard, Duke of York

53 **one false glass** Richard, who does not look like his father. This is an important point because Richard will later base his claim to the throne on his resemblance to his father. Throughout the play the villain uses his outward appearance in hypocritical and deceptive ways

121 **Ludlow** an important castle was built at Ludlow in Shropshire. Prince Edward and his retinue were based there at the time of Edward IV's death

127 **the estate is green** the country is fragile and easily damaged, like a young plant. The use of 'green' also implies the young prince is innocent and untested, not yet ready to rule. It is one of the natural images used to depict the perilous state of England while it is under Richard's influence (see Imagery). It is repeated at line 135

SCENE 3   Citizens discuss the fate of England after Edward's death

Three citizens discuss the news that Edward is dead. The first citizen is optimistic about the future, while his companions are less sure. The third citizen is particularly troubled and pessimistic. He believes that Richard is treacherous and has little faith in Elizabeth's relatives either. He predicts woe for a country which has a child for its monarch. The second citizen echoes his gloomy tone when he says that 'the hearts of men are full of fear' (line 38).

The plot is not developed in this scene, which has a **choric** function. The citizens' uneasiness – in particular the third citizen's sense of foreboding – mirrors the misery and dread seen in the previous scene. We are also being encouraged to see the wider impact of Edward's death. It is not simply one family which suffers when a king dies. Shakespeare is quite explicit about the historical and political consequences of Edward IV's death, and again recent events are linked to the past, suggesting a cycle of woe. There are verbal links between this scene and the previous one, particularly in the third citizen's use of **metaphor** at line 33; in Act II Scene 2 Elizabeth asked two agonised rhetorical questions: 'Why grow the branches, when the root is gone? / Why wither not the leaves that want their sap?' (II.2.41–2). Her remarks had personal resonance only; now the third citizen makes it plain that everyone in England is affected: 'When great leaves fall, then winter is at hand' (line 33). The prophecies made in this scene can also be linked to the Duchess of York's pronouncements in both Act II Scene 2 and the following scene. Finally, it is appropriate that we see the distrust Richard is held in by the populace at this point. We are being prepared for the scene when Richard seizes the throne in London, observed by an uneasy crowd.

4 **by'rlady; seldom comes the better** proverbial, meaning that change usually signals the worst
6 **God speed** a common greeting at the time, meaning may God make you prosper
11 **Woe to the land ... child** a proverb taken from Ecclesiastes 10:16

SCENE 4   **Elizabeth resolves to go into sanctuary with her young son when she learns that members of her family have been arrested**

Elizabeth, her son the young Duke of York, the Duchess of York and the Archbishop of York await the arrival of Prince Edward. Richard's prodigious birth is discussed. A messenger arrives with news that Rivers, Vaughan and Grey have been arrested on Richard and Buckingham's orders and taken to Pomfret Castle. Elizabeth and the Duchess of York condemn this act of tyranny, deciding to take sanctuary with the young duke. Elizabeth fears the destruction of her family.

> Like Act II Scene 2, this scene opens with a child, the witty and 'parlous' (line 35) Duke of York. Unlike Clarence's children, this child and his brother Edward have individual characteristics, making the pathos of their deaths more affecting. Like his cousin, little York seems to have been influenced by Richard. He, however, is less trusting and more sardonic than Clarence's boy. York's and the duchess's descriptions of Richard's monstrous infancy are designed to repulse us and remind us how unnatural he is. These stories of Richard were common currency in the Elizabethan period, part of the Tudor myth that is discussed in Critical Approaches.
>
> The duchess reminds us of the past – and the fate of usurpers – when she says, 'My husband lost his life to get the crown' (line 57). It is clear that the cycle of misery is continuing and ceaseless: Elizabeth's kindred have been imprisoned. Further dire and ponderous prophecies add to the sense of ritual; fate is being played out in *Richard III*. The formal rhetoric of the women contrasts with the conversational tone of the early part of the scene. This is appropriate now that events have taken a sinister turn. The women are united in grief by this point, seeking sanctuary together, just as Richard's enemies will unite in Act IV. When Elizabeth calls Richard a 'tiger' (line 50) she adds to the list of savage and repellent animal metaphors Shakespeare uses to characterise his villain throughout the play. By the end of Act II Margaret's warnings have proved sound and we know there is worse to come.

s.d. **young Duke of York** Richard was the younger son of Elizabeth and Edward, aged ten at this time

1 **Stony Stratford** a town in Buckinghamshire, north of London

2 **Northampton** a larger town near Stony Stratford. Richard and Buckingham are deliberately taking a circuitous route so that the Woodevilles can be arrested and kept away from the young prince

13 **'Small herbs ... apace'** a proverb

37 **Pitchers have ears** a pitcher's ears are its handles. The saying means that it is important to be careful what you say because there may be people listening

42 **Pomfret** a castle and town in Yorkshire. Richard II was imprisoned and killed here. We are being reminded of the destructive cycle which began with his usurpation

43 **Sir Thomas Vaughan** chamberlain to Prince Edward, an important post. He was a supporter of the Woodeville faction and therefore dangerous to Richard

66 **sanctuary** a holy place where people could take refuge and avoid arrest. Elizabeth takes sanctuary at Westminster Abbey

71 **seal** the Lord Chancellor, who was at this time the Archbishop of York, was given possession of the Great Seal of England by Edward IV before he died. It was illegal for him to give the seal to Elizabeth, making this a highly political act

ACT III

SCENE 1 **Prince Edward arrives in London. Richard and Buckingham send Catesby to find out if Hastings will support Richard in his bid for the throne**

When he arrives in London with his uncle Richard and Buckingham, Prince Edward seems discontented. He is not convinced that his uncles were as treacherous as Gloucester tells him they were, and he wants to know where his mother and brother are. The Lord Mayor greets him and Hastings enters with the news that Elizabeth and young York have taken sanctuary. Buckingham urges the Cardinal to fetch York and he takes Hastings with him in his mission to persuade Elizabeth to part with her child. Prince Edward is told that he will be lodging at the Tower until his coronation. He is uneasy about going there. York is brought in by Hastings and the Cardinal. He jests with Richard, but is also disconcerted when he learns that he will be staying at the Tower. The boys are led off and Richard and Buckingham discuss their plans with Catesby, who is asked to sound out Hastings. They wish to know whether he will support Richard when he seizes the crown. Richard tells Buckingham that Hastings must die if he refuses to support him. He promises his accomplice the earldom of Hereford when he succeeds to the throne.

In contrast to his witty and lively brother, Edward initially seems a gloomy and petulant child. However, we recognise that he is right to have a heavy heart: his uncles have been imprisoned, his mother and brother have not come to London to greet him and the Tower is not an auspicious place to start one's reign. We also recognise the boy's valour when he says he hopes to regain the lands lost in France. Here Shakespeare offers us a glimpse of what might have been; the pathos and **irony** of the boy's utterances are poignant. There is further irony of a more sinister kind when young York arrives. He and Edward mock their uncle, who, we are well aware, will have the last laugh. Richard's murderous intentions are revealed in his proverbial **aside** at line 79 and then in wordplay at lines 111, 122 and 135. His 'jokes' become more threatening each time. The contrast between the princes' innocent high spirits and Richard's diabolical **double entendres** adds dramatic tension to the scene, as does the contrast between Edward's melancholy and Richard's and Buckingham's false bonhomie in the opening lines.

The princes are not the only dupes in this scene. Indeed, they are less foolish than both Hastings and the Cardinal, who allow themselves to be manipulated too easily. The Cardinal seems particularly weak. Buckingham continues to use the same sort of verbose rationalisations he employed in Act II Scene 2, but he does not conceal his power; in fact, he seems to be more assured and firm in 'mine opinion' (line 52), taking the lead when he insists that York must be plucked 'perforce' (line 36) from sanctuary. Richard does not play any significant part in the manoeuvrings that occur in this scene until the conversation with Catesby, and even here he says less than Buckingham. This is clearly a political decision: he cannot afford to reveal his hand too directly. Instead he uses Buckingham to get what he wants. In return for his support, he promises great wealth as a reward. It seems appropriate that these two schemers should use a double agent, Catesby, who professes to be Hastings's friend, to further their plans. But Buckingham's self-confidence is misplaced. Richard's startling words at line 193 confirm *his* brutal control of events. Buckingham wonders how they should deal with Hastings if he will not support them. 'Chop off his head, man' is the brisk, callous reply. This is how Richard deals with all his enemies: Buckingham, beware.

It is worth considering Richard's theatrical and self-conscious reference to the '**Vice**, Iniquity' at line 82. Here the villain does not seem to see the limitations of the role he has chosen. The Vice was always vanquished in the dramas in which he appeared; too clever for his own good, the witty devil could never win. So Richard's boast is empty. He is trapped by his villainy even as he revels in it, as he does here. At the same time, it is impossible for us not to be entertained by the Vice. When he toys with his nephews, Richard's humour may be alarming, but it is compelling in a way that Buckingham's **Machiavellian** posturing is not. We are still caught in a curious position in Act III; while abhorring the villain and acknowledging the misery and suffering he is responsible for, we are still drawn to his knowing evil. This will change in Act IV.

s.d. **Lord Cardinal [Bourchier]** Thomas Bourchier was Archbishop of Canterbury

69 **Julius Caesar** the Roman general and statesman who twice invaded Britain. It was erroneously believed that he had begun building the Tower of London

78 **the general all-ending day** Judgement Day

79 **So wise so young, they say, do never live long** proverbial

82 **the formal Vice, Iniquity** a stock character from the medieval morality plays (see Characterisation). Richard draws attention to his own performance here

92 **our ancient right in France** the kings of England had made many concerted efforts to capture lands in France and exert a claim to the French throne since 1340. Henry V had a famous victory at Agincourt, while his son Henry VI was crowned king of France as well as England. During Henry VI's reign Britain lost all its French territories, except for Calais

130 **like an ape** the boy is mocking his uncle Richard by calling attention to his crookback. Monkeys were kept for amusement, sometimes being put on their owners' shoulders

154 **parlous** talkative; the word also has the suggestion of perilous

SCENE 2   **Hastings makes it clear that he will not support Richard. He does not believe that he is dangerous. Catesby, Stanley and Hastings make their way to the Tower**

The scene opens with a sense of urgency as a messenger from Lord Stanley raps on Hastings's door at four o'clock in the morning. He has come to report an ominous dream that his master has had. Believing that Richard is treacherous and means to harm them, Stanley wants Hastings to flee to the north with him. Hastings dismisses this idea and tells the messenger to return to Stanley; they should both proceed to the Tower, where they will take part in a council meeting. Catesby arrives. He has come to find out whether Hastings will support Richard. He also informs him that his old enemies, Queen Elizabeth's relatives, are to be put to death at Pomfret. Hastings is glad to hear this news, but he refuses to support Richard. Stanley enters, still brooding over 'these several Councils' (line 75). Nevertheless, he allows himself to be persuaded to go 'toward the Tower' (line 116) for the meeting. Buckingham appears briefly at the end of the scene, also on his way to the Tower.

> Stanley's dream, in which the boar (Richard) 'razed off his helm' (line 10), is as accurately prophetic as the other dreams in this play. And it is not the only warning Hastings receives in this scene. He is presented with two pieces of information that should make him less trusting: firstly, that there are to be two separate council meetings; secondly, that Richard has begun to eliminate his enemies. It is **ironic** that Hastings is pleased when he learns that Rivers, Grey and Vaughan are to be executed. Can he not see the danger he is in when he refuses to support Richard? No, he cannot. His logic is foolish. He complacently believes that 'the boar will use' him 'kindly' (line 32), even though he states – rashly – that he believes the crown would be 'foul misplac'd' (line 43) on Richard's head. He misses the irony in Catesby's prophetic words at line 61, ignores Stanley's further warnings, and does not recognise the

veiled threat Buckingham offers at line 113. Catesby's and Buckingham's Ricardian asides seal Hastings's fate. Because these asides refer to the impending death of a character onstage, they link this scene to the previous one, in which Richard's murderous intentions towards his nephews were established. The repeated references to the fate of the prisoners at Pomfret serve two purposes. They prepare us for the scene that follows, while also foreshadowing Hastings's own end. The scene ends with a reference to supper, which also links this scene to Act III Scene 1. In both, meals are the prelude to death. Hastings's jovial mood is as inappropriate as young York's. But, having already been imprisoned in the Tower, he should know better than to trust the house of York. So far Richard's victims have been easy prey. Does this diminish the villain's stature?

10 **razed off** scrape or cut off, erase

helm helmet

69 **the Bridge** London Bridge, where the heads of traitors were displayed on poles

107 **Sir John** a clergyman who had taken his first degree used the title 'Sir'

113 **shriving work** shrift, confession. Condemned prisoners were customarily allowed to confess their sins and ask for absolution before they were executed. Buckingham, who knows what Hastings's fate will be, is making a black joke

120 **And supper too** more irony at Hastings's expense. Hastings will not leave the Tower at all: he will be executed there. References to eating become a running joke in the play. Eventually the joke is on Richard because he loses his appetite the night before the battle on Bosworth field

SCENE 3   Rivers, Grey and Vaughan are put to death at Pomfret

Elizabeth's kindred are led to execution. As they go they make further prophecies of woe, and recall the death of Richard II, who was usurped and put to death at Pomfret. They remember Margaret's curses, and Rivers, like Clarence before him, hopes that God will not avenge Himself on his family further but will spare the lives of Elizabeth and her sons.

Like Act II Scene 3, this scene has a **choric** function and shows the way in which Shakespeare telescopes time in *Richard III*. Rivers,

Grey and Vaughan lament the downfall of their house by recalling the past and making predictions about the future, again locating events in the cycle of history that is being played out. Rivers's hopes are sadly **ironic**: we know the princes will not be spared. The reference to Margaret confirms the accuracy of her judgement and suggests there is worse to come for the characters mentioned by Rivers. Some critics have suggested that this scene is a turning point in the play: the predictions made in Act I Scene 3 are proving true. Richard's relentless rise is confirmed by the several downfalls that occur in this act. However, we know he will not be triumphant for long. Many Elizabethans believed that it was Richard II's death that led – indirectly – to the Wars of the Roses, and that the victory of Henry VII and the Tudor dynasty put a just end to the cycle of evil that began when Henry Bolingbroke (Henry IV) usurped Richard's throne.

12 **Richard the Second** Richard was murdered at Pomfret in 1400. In reality he was probably starved to death

SCENE 4   **At the council meeting Richard accuses Hastings of treachery and orders his execution**

The council meeting opens with Hastings asking when the new king will be crowned. He is confident that Richard trusts and loves him, and that he can speak for him. When he arrives Richard seems relaxed and friendly, asking the Bishop of Ely to send for some strawberries from his garden. It quickly becomes clear that these are diversionary tactics. Richard takes Buckingham to one side to discuss Hastings's fate, while the rest of the council continue to discuss the coronation. When he returns, Richard's tone has changed. He is angry, accusing Mistress Shore and Elizabeth of using witchcraft against him, and Hastings of treachery. He commands Lovell and Ratcliffe to execute Hastings immediately. Hastings is left alone to bewail his fate and folly while the rest of the council take their leave with Richard.

This short but dramatic scene shows Richard's inexorable progress towards the crown. Hastings's downfall has been dwelt on in a very focused way during this act. Like Gloucester's other victims, he realises the truth too late and can only make wise prophecies about the future when he is close to death. At the beginning of the scene it is clear that Buckingham is speaking **ironically**, and again the foolish Hastings misses a warning (lines 10–13). Richard's request for strawberries seems laughably trivial, but we recognise his indirect but cunning methods of manipulation. He is lulling his audience into a false sense of security.

Unsurprisingly, the council members seem unable to deal with Gloucester throughout the scene. After Hastings's protestations nobody attempts to thwart him and the lords hurry off in Richard's wake without a word. Are they scared? Their failure to stand up to Richard shows how evil proceeds unchecked when men are weak and gullible. The meeting is a meaningless ritual which Richard subverts completely with his unsubstantiated accusations (this is not to underplay the accusations of witchcraft, which the Elizabethans continued to believe in). His lightning change of mood is as effective and bewildering as it was in Act I Scene 3 and Act II Scene 1. The fact that he succeeds in achieving his ends with wild lies shows his increasing power, as does the swiftness of Hastings's downfall. Ratcliffe's cruel taunts at line 95 round off the repeated references to supper time in a particularly brutal way. For an extended commentary on part of this scene see Text 1 in Textual Analysis.

31 **Holborn** a district in west London. The bishops of Ely had Ely House in Holborn at their disposal

69 **blasted sapling** it was well known that Richard was deformed from birth. This natural image aptly conveys the villain's corruption

84 **foot-cloth horse** a horse with trappings that came down over its sides, covering the rider's feet

SCENE 5   **The Mayor is persuaded to explain to the citizens that Hastings was executed in a just cause. Richard continues to scheme against his brothers' children while Buckingham speaks to the crowd in favour of Richard's accession**

Richard and Buckingham discuss their tactics for dealing with the Mayor. They counterfeit fear, pretending to be beset by enemies. The

Mayor is taken in by their story that Hastings plotted against their lives, agreeing to explain to the citizens of London why he was put to death without trial. Richard sends Buckingham after him. He is to address the crowd too, inferring 'the bastardy of Edward's children' (line 74) and impugning the Duchess of York's virtue. The aim is to make the citizens believe that Richard is the only rightful heir to the throne. Meanwhile Gloucester will repair to Baynard's Castle where he will gather religious men around him in order to establish the appearance of unworldly piety. At the end of the scene Richard is plotting against Clarence's children as well as the princes.

A great deal is set up and outlined in this short scene. Richard's virtuosity as an actor is demonstrated a number of times. He plays many roles with relish: acting coach, frightened innocent, grieving friend, righteous Lord Protector of the realm and scheming, opportunistic **Machiavel**. He also prepares for his next role: that of pious churchman. Again, we can only marvel at his swift and brilliant changes in tone and mastery of words. There is a good deal of humour in this scene, from the moment Richard and Buckingham enter in their ridiculous '*rotten armour*'. The Mayor is as feeble as the Cardinal and the council, easily dazzled by the dissemblers who bombard him verbally. Buckingham and Richard make an entertaining double act as they woo him with false protestations. When they are alone together, however, we see how much Buckingham relies on Richard, who tells him what to say and how to say it. Buckingham, foolishly, remains complacent about his own powers, as his speeches at lines 5 and 94 show. Richard's decisive speech that closes the scene confirms the villain's control of events.

40 **Turks or infidels** Turk was a byword for cruel tyranny. Like other 'heathens', the Turks were believed to treat their captives in unjust and barbaric ways

72 **Guildhall** the Guildhall was the official meeting place for the citizens of London

97 **Baynard's Castle** one of Richard's London residences, situated on the Thames between Blackfriars and London Bridge

102–3 **Doctor Shaa … Friar Penker** Shaa was the Lord Mayor's brother. He and Penker, an Augustine friar, were famous preachers who supported Richard

105 **privy order** an arrangement made in secret

SCENE 6 **The scrivener describes how he began writing out the indictment several hours before Hastings was declared a traitor**

The scrivener holds a copy of the indictment of Hastings in his hand, which he spent eleven hours writing. Catesby delivered it to him for copying 'yesternight' (line 6), so it was clearly composed before Hastings was accused of treason at the council meeting. The scrivener says that the 'palpable device' (line 11) should be evident to all, but he acknowledges that a man would be foolish to speak the truth.

> Like the third citizen in Act II Scene 3, the scrivener is critical of the regime that is taking over. His negative attitude **foreshadows** the uneasy silence that will prevail when Buckingham addresses the crowd in the next scene. But his rhetorical questions at lines 10–12 demonstrate the difficulty of opposing Richard. The rhyming couplet that closes the scene provides another gloomy prediction. We will not be surprised to learn of the double-dealing Catesby's role in Hastings's downfall. He will play an important role in Act III Scene 7 too.

s.d. **Scrivener** a scrivener or scribe was an official copyist

11 **palpable device** obvious trick

SCENE 7 **Richard pretends to be reluctant to take the crown. Buckingham urges him to listen to a deputation. Richard is proclaimed king**

The citizens of London have not received Buckingham's oration joyfully. Instead of supporting Richard's claim to the throne they have remained silent. The only men who have responded enthusiastically are Buckingham's followers, who have been planted in the crowd. Nonetheless, Richard remains convinced that he will triumph. The Mayor and aldermen have come to persuade him to take the crown. When he appears he is flanked by two bishops, reading from a prayer book. Richard feigns reluctance to hear the deputation. Then he says that he is unworthy to be king because of his 'poverty of spirit' and 'defects' (lines 158–9). Buckingham urges him to think again; Prince Edward is a bastard and cannot succeed his father. He threatens to 'plant some other in the throne' (line 215) if Richard does not capitulate, and haughtily declares that he will 'entreat no more' (line 218). Buckingham leads off the Mayor and the aldermen while Catesby urges 'sweet Prince' Richard to 'accept their suit' (line 220). Sighing about having 'a world of cares' (line 222) thrust upon him, Richard gracefully gives in and is saluted with his new royal title. He agrees to be crowned the next day at Buckingham's suggestion and leaves the stage pretending that he wishes to continue with his religious devotions.

> The longest scene in Act III is a masterpiece of hypocritical posturing. What we see is almost a play within a play. Catesby and Buckingham act their assigned roles with gusto, but it is Richard who really impresses as an actor. He is reluctant and unworldly, making excellent use of the bishops, who serve as props. The gullible Mayor unwittingly plays his role as supporting actor too. Buckingham and Richard use rhetoric to dissemble, employing long sentences and relative clauses to build up their arguments. Richard's public tone is measured and formal, contrasting with the blunt and energetic style he uses in private with Buckingham at the start of the scene ('What, tongueless blocks were they? Would they not speak!' line 42). He employs poetic **metaphors** and **images** in his long speech at line 140 when he outlines his reluctance to take the throne, creating an impression of a humble, wise and gracious individual who prefers religion to politics. You will notice, however, that he cleverly avoids absolutely declining the throne here, preferring to say 'there is no need of me' (line 164). This not only gives him the option of accepting later on, but also leaves the way open for Buckingham to explain why the country *does* in fact need him. It is extremely **ironic** that Buckingham makes much of Richard's conscience in his speech at line 173, for two reasons. Firstly, Richard is entirely without conscience at this point; secondly, we know that he will be forced to face up to his own evil deeds before he dies. It is also ironic that Buckingham's talk

of conscience immediately precedes a slanderous description of Elizabeth's past; the henchman has no conscience either. Thereafter, there is conscious and unconscious irony in almost every word uttered. Richard is indeed 'unfit for state and majesty' (line 204), as we are only too well aware. He is 'made of stones' (line 223). But at this moment Gloucester is outrageously knowing and sure of himself, as his speech at line 222 shows. Here he even makes jokes about his deformity and the 'black scandal' (line 230) that will attach itself to his reign. Surely this kind of mocking pride must come before a fall? This is a scene of visual and verbal distortions of the truth which shows Richard at the zenith of his powers, a fitting end to three acts of devilish plotting.

5 **Lady Lucy** Sir Thomas More is the source for the story that Edward was engaged to Lady Elizabeth Lucy before he married Elizabeth Grey. If there was an engagement it meant that his marriage to Queen Elizabeth was not legal, and therefore his offspring were illegitimate and not true heirs to the throne of England

6 **contract ... in France** as well as the doubts about his relationship with Lady Lucy, there are further aspersions to be cast about a match that was negotiated with King Louis XI of France in 1464 between Edward and the sister of the French queen, Lady Bona of Savoy. A betrothal did not take place, in spite of what Buckingham says here. But the situation was awkward enough and caused a good deal of political disruption and scandal. While the negotiations were still taking place Edward married Elizabeth Grey in secret

15 **victories in Scotland** in 1482 Richard led the capture of Berwick. He had a very successful career as a soldier before he became king

30 **the Recorder** the civil magistrate of the city of London, Thomas Fitzwilliam

50 **Play the maid's part** proverb. To say no when you really mean yes

182 **poor petitioner** Queen Elizabeth. A reference to the scene in *3 Henry VI* when Elizabeth first meets Edward. They met when she came to petition him about an inheritance

188 **bigamy** according to canon law, marriage with a widow was bigamy. If either of the contracts with Lady Lucy or Bona of Savoy were valid, then this would also make the match with Elizabeth Grey bigamous

ACT IV

SCENE 1   **Elizabeth, the Duchess of York and Anne are refused admittance to the Tower. They learn that Richard is king**

As the scene opens the three women and Clarence's daughter are on their way to visit the princes in the Tower. Dorset accompanies them. Brakenbury, Lord Lieutenant of the Tower, refuses to admit them: King Richard has decreed that the boys must be kept in isolation. Brakenbury is deaf to the women's pleas. Stanley comes to tell Anne that she must prepare for the coronation. Elizabeth swoons and tells her son Dorset that he must flee to Richmond in France if he is to save his head. Stanley agrees that this is wise counsel. It becomes clear that he and his son are opposed to Richard. All the women lament Richard's accession. They are united in grief. Anne says that her husband suffers 'timorous dreams' (line 84) and she fears that he will shortly be rid of her. As she makes her leave, Elizabeth looks back at the Tower, deeply concerned about the fate of her young sons.

> The women are characteristically sorrowful in this scene. Now, however, they find time to pity one another, instead of competing in their grief. Anne is a particularly pathetic figure as she recounts the sorry tale of her wooing and marriage. She predicts her own death and seems to welcome it. Elizabeth, the unhappy mother, is a figure of great pathos too. Her final speech is very poignant. The Tower has come to be a monstrous symbol of Richard's evil. There are many concrete **images** of blood and destruction in this scene which demonstrate the intensity of feeling onstage, as well as pointing to the grim future of England under Richard's rule. Elizabeth's description of the realm as a 'slaughter-house' (line 43) is arresting, as is Anne's desire to be seared to the brains with 'red-hot steel' (line 60). However, we see clear signs of opposition emerging. Not only are the women united, but it also seems that Stanley is preparing to revolt against his usurping sovereign. Even Brakenbury seems embarrassed about his oath of allegiance to Richard, reverting to the term 'Lord Protector' when Elizabeth corrects him at line 18. As critics have suggested, Margaret's role of prophetess of doom has been assumed by the Duchess of York. She

continues to lament the fact that she ever gave birth to Richard, and has great dignity as she bids the other women farewell with kind wishes. We know that her hopes are fragile, but this does not detract from the solemnity of the scene.

42 **Richmond** Richmond was taken to France by his uncle Jasper Tudor after the Lancastrian defeat at Tewkesbury in 1471. He was fourteen years old at this time

54 **cockatrice** a serpent, which was identified with the basilisk (see I.2.154) because its glance was mortal

61 **Anointed** a reference to Medea's murder of Creon's daughter, Creusa, in Seneca's *Medea*. Creusa was anointed with poison and died when she put on a poisoned coronet sent to her by Medea

69 **that dear saint** Henry VI, who was well known for his piety

SCENE *2*   **Buckingham prevaricates when asked to arrange the murder of the young princes in the Tower. Tyrrel agrees to undertake the task. Buckingham takes flight**

Richard ascends the throne. His thoughts immediately turn to murder. When Buckingham fails to understand his hints, he is forced to tell him plainly that he wants the princes in the Tower killed. Buckingham asks for time to consider this proposition, angering his sovereign. Richard decides to find another murderer he can bribe. His page suggests that a 'discontented gentleman' (line 36), Tyrrel, is his man. Stanley brings news that Dorset has fled to Richmond. Richard tells Catesby to put out rumours that Anne is sick and likely to die soon; he intends to marry Elizabeth's eldest daughter in order to strengthen his position. Tyrrel arrives and agrees to murder the princes. When Buckingham reappears he swiftly realises that his days are numbered. He attempts to remind Richard that he was promised the earldom of Hereford, but is told that the king is 'not in the giving vein today' (line 116). Richard is preoccupied by a prophecy that he 'should not live long after I saw "Richmond"' (line 105). At the end of the scene the fearful Buckingham decides to flee to Brecknock in Wales.

This is a highly dramatic and swift-moving scene. It becomes clear that Richard is already past his zenith. He is forced to respond to unwelcome news and setbacks. For the first time he gives voice to doubts, although he remains decisive and brutal. The first hint of uncertainty comes at line 5. Although it is clear that Richard believes he is speaking rhetorically, preparing to prime Buckingham for the murder of the princes, his question has serious implications. As the scene progresses we realise that the sovereign is not secure. His henchman hesitates, Dorset has fled and Richard recognises that he must marry again if he is to maintain his authority. Finally, and most significantly, he seems to be taking prophecies seriously now. Richard has none of his old mocking humour in this scene. He is simply sinister. And he is isolated. The two exchanges with Buckingham show this. The men talk at cross purposes, and although Richard is clearly in control in the second conversation, this is not true of the first. Buckingham forces him to reconsider his tactics. The syntax of some of Richard's speeches also suggests agitation, especially from line 80 onwards.

The villain seems determined to keep moving forward on his destructive course, however. He reiterates the choice he made in Act I Scene 1, although we might sense a hint of reluctance in his words: 'But I am in / So far in blood that sin will pluck on sin' (lines 63–4). 'But' suggests that he is girding his loins, forcing himself not to waver in his purpose. What has happened to Richard's delight in evil for its own sake? Some critics have suggested that the protagonist does not know what to do once he has achieved the crown. What was all his scheming for? He has no grand design for England, merely an egotistical desire to remain on the throne he has usurped. Act IV Scene 2 suggests that Richard has no future because the present is so uncertain, a direct result of the sins he committed in the past.

It is **ironic** that Buckingham should appeal to Richard's 'honour and ... faith' (line 88) when he tries to claim the inheritance that he was promised. Surely he must know that his sovereign possesses neither of these qualities? These words clearly **foreshadow** Buckingham's fall.

18 **the bastards** the princes in the Tower. It is intriguing that Richard refers to the boys as 'bastards' even when he is speaking to Buckingham, who helped

him concoct the story about their illegitimacy. Why does he maintain the lie with his corrupt ally? Does this show the lengths to which Richard will go to foster the appearance of his own legitimacy? Or is this a sign of the villain's growing weakness because he can no longer speak honestly to anyone?

28 **iron-witted** dull-witted, stupid

55 **The boy** Clarence's son

60 **my brother's daughter** Elizabeth and Edward's eldest daughter, Elizabeth of York

114 **jack** the figure of the man who strikes the bell on the outside of a clock; the term also means a scoundrel

122 **Brecknock** Brecon, Buckingham's family seat in South Wales

SCENE 3   **Tyrrel describes the murder of the princes and informs Richard that they are dead. Ely and Buckingham have deserted the king, who prepares for war**

Tyrrel offers a vivid and poignant description of the princes' deaths. It is clear that the two men he procured to commit the murders already regret their actions. By way of contrast, Richard reacts coolly when he hears the news. He outlines his most recent plots. Ratcliffe brings news that Richmond is gathering support and Buckingham leads an army of Welshmen.

> Richard seems to have regained his composure in this scene, even if he remains restless. But time is moving swiftly on and he cannot afford to be complacent. Anne's death, the marriage of Clarence's daughter and the Buckingham rebellion are all dealt with perfunctorily. The fact that Richard does not waste words on these events suggests the villain's callousness. The princes, however, receive a moving epitaph from Tyrrel. His words are poetic and lyrical, and the incorporation of direct speech adds to the horror and pathos of the report. Dighton and Forrest highlight the theme of conscience again, preparing us for the scene in which Richard confronts his own dark soul in Act V. For the moment, however, he is confident and unabashed as he prepares to play the 'jolly thriving wooer' (line 43) again. He does not seem alarmed at having to make preparations for war. As we shall see, Richard III is undoubtedly a brave soldier.

11 **alabaster** a figure on a tomb; alabaster is a smooth white stone. Shakespeare commonly uses this **image** to depict sleeping figures before they die

19 **prime creation** the beginning of the world. The religious reference here shows us the importance of the death of the princes

38 **Abraham's bosom** heaven

46 **Morton** John Morton, Bishop of Ely

55 **Jove's Mercury** Richard reveals his interest in appearances again, speaking of the heraldry he wishes to use when he goes onto the battlefield. Jove is the king of the gods in Roman mythology, while Mercury is his herald

SCENE 4 **Margaret gloats over Elizabeth's misfortunes. Richard tries to persuade Elizabeth to help him woo her daughter. He continues with his preparations to fight Richmond**

Margaret listens at the side of the stage as Elizabeth and the Duchess of York lament their misfortunes, making acidic comments. She revels in her enemies' misery. When she steps forward she is as vengeful as she was in Act I. Having mocked Elizabeth and the duchess, she announces her intention to leave for France. The two grieving women who remain intercept Richard with accusations. The Duchess of York curses her son and predicts a bloody end for him. Richard then attempts to persuade Elizabeth that she should allow him to marry her eldest daughter, Elizabeth of York. After a long confrontation Elizabeth appears to concur with the plan.

Ratcliffe brings bad news: Richmond is sailing to Wales and continues to gather support. Stanley confirms this report. Richard, who is suspicious of Stanley, makes him leave his son behind as a hostage when he goes to rally troops. Further messengers bring bad tidings of rebellions in Devon, Kent and Yorkshire. At the end of the scene Richard learns that Buckingham has been captured and his army dispersed. Conflicting reports of Richmond's whereabouts follow one another, but it seems that he has landed at Milford Haven in Wales. Richard immediately prepares to march to Salisbury with his army. He wants the captive Buckingham brought there.

The furious pace at which the final part of scene proceeds and the conflicting reports that arrive show that Richard's downfall is approaching swiftly. Before the hectic action of the messenger scene, however, we watch two essentially static encounters. Margaret's reappearance and departure to France are an integral part of the final lamentation scene of *Richard III*. Her vengeful, bitter words propel Elizabeth and the Duchess of York towards a powerful confrontation with Richard. As Elizabeth suggests, the vicious old queen has taught them how to curse. It is important that the women are allowed to give their passionate feelings a final outlet, and appropriate that they remind us – and Richard – of Richard's crimes; we must not forget that the villain has achieved power through his abuse and murder of women and children. In Act V both Richmond and Richard will appeal to their soldiers' protective feelings towards their wives and children. Here the women remind us that the most vulnerable members of society, most particularly the villain's own family, are not safe while Richard reigns. The women's lamentations again draw our attention to the cycles of history, of sin and expiation, that have characterised the Wars of the Roses. The bloody **imagery** they use reinforces their grim message. The repetitive phrasing that Shakespeare incorporates is powerful and insistent, as are the vituperative **metaphors** that are invoked as the women denounce Richard. The Duchess of York's last lines are as firm as Margaret's and again we recognise the wisdom and justice of her prophecy. Richard, the 'hell-hound' (line 48), deserves to meet a bloody and violent end.

But what are we to make of the second part of the scene, Richard's 'wooing' of Elizabeth? Strangely, this encounter is longer than Richard's seduction of Anne. Is the villain losing his touch? Most assuredly, yes. Elizabeth proves to be an able, rational and bitter opponent. Richard is not able to gain control of this conversation and win over his listener so easily. Elizabeth interrupts, she twists Richard's words and deliberately misunderstands him. She has answers, asks questions and confronts the villain with his crimes very forcefully. Her tone is often sarcastic and sardonic, like Richard's was early in the play. We cannot be absolutely sure that Elizabeth has wholeheartedly capitulated to her brother-in-law. Her question at line 426 leaves us doubtful, even though Richard believes he has won. His triumph will be very short-lived; in the next scene we learn that Elizabeth of York is to be Richmond's bride.

Richard's gradual loss of control is also demonstrated during the messenger scene. He undoubtedly remains a powerful and compelling figure here, and retains his mental toughness, but when he strikes the third messenger his agitation is graphically demonstrated. **Ironically** this messenger brings one of the few pieces of good news. Richard's uncertainty is also expressed through his use of questions and exclamations. At the end of the scene he recovers some of his power in his decisive final lines. The scene is set for the 'royal battle' (line 536). Richard will go down fighting. His encounter with Elizabeth has shown us that he does not give up, even when the odds are against him. For an extended commentary on part of this scene see Text 2 in Textual Analysis.

49 **had his teeth** legend has it that Richard was born with teeth – another sign of his monstrous nature

251 **Lethe** from Greek mythology. The Lethe was a river in the underworld. Anyone who drank from its waters immediately forgot the past

336 **Caesar's Caesar** Roman emperors used Julius Caesar's name as a title

346 **the King's King** God forbade brothers from marrying each other's daughters – it was incest

366 **my George, my Garter** St George is the patron saint of England. Knights of the Garter (the highest order of English knighthood) wear a jewel which has an image of St George on it. Here – ironically, since he has devastated the royal family – Richard seems to be insisting on his own chivalry and patriotism

464 **White-liver'd** cowardly

SCENE 5   **Stanley cannot support Richmond openly because his son is being held hostage by Richard. Elizabeth has agreed that her daughter should marry Richmond**

Stanley sends Sir Christopher Urswick to Richmond with the news that his son is 'frank'd up in hold' (line 3) by Richard. As a result he is unable to declare his support for Richmond openly, or send him any 'present aid' (line 5). He also asks Urswick to inform him that Elizabeth has consented to the match between her daughter and Richmond. Stanley asks about Richmond's whereabouts and is informed that he is in Wales, and has gained the support of a number of important English noblemen.

This short, flat scene clarifies Stanley's position and provides two important pieces of information. Richmond continues to gain ground, and Elizabeth has chosen to support his cause, promising him her daughter's hand in marriage. After the intensity of the previous scene, a moment's respite is welcome before the battle begins.

2 **sty** a reference to Richard's heraldic symbol, the boar

10 **Pembroke ... Ha'rfordwest** towns in South Wales. By this point we realise that Richard's enemies are closing in on him

ACT V

SCENE 1 **Buckingham is led to his death**

Buckingham's fatalistic speeches have some of the qualities of a **choric** lament. He sees the justice of his death, appealing to the souls of the dead and recalling the events of the past which have led him to his destiny. But he also points to the future when he mentions Margaret's curse. We know that Richard will shortly be afflicted by the guilt and conscience that preoccupy Buckingham here. Another foolish man sees the truth too late. You might feel that Richard's dream of Act V Scene 3 is **foreshadowed** by the references to the villain's earlier victims.

10 **All-Souls' day** Judgement Day. The second of November is a day when Christians remember the dead. The reference implies Buckingham's penitence

25 **Margaret's curse** made in I.3.299–300

SCENE 2 **Richmond and his supporters set out to fight Richard's forces near Leicester**

Richmond offers a stirring oration, urging his supporters to fight in God's name for 'perpetual peace' (line 15). He is marching on Tamworth, where he hopes to meet Richard in battle. Herbert and Oxford share their leader's good spirits. Stanley has sent a letter of 'comfort and encouragement' (line 6).

> This is an optimistic scene. Richmond is as resolute as Richard, and speaks with the gracious ceremony that becomes a victor. Important themes are mentioned here: conscience, guilt and God's justice. Richard's vilification as the 'wretched, bloody, and usurping boar' (line 7) who has destroyed England's peace is continued. From the moment that he appears we are aware that Richmond is being presented as the saviour of the realm, who has the Almighty on his side.

12 **Leicester** a town in the east Midlands, north of London

13 **Tamworth** a town twenty miles from Leicester

SCENE 3   **The rival armies pitch their tents near Market Bosworth. The ghosts of Richard's victims appear and speak to Richard and Richmond in their dreams. The battle begins the next morning**

Richard and his supporters pitch their tents in Bosworth field. Richard attempts to cheer Norfolk and Surrey, who looks downcast. He enquires about the strength of the enemy and is pleased to learn that his own army is considerably larger. He sets out to make a survey of the battlefield. Observing the sunset, Richmond declares it is a good omen. He organises his supporters and retires to his tent to draw up his battle plans with Brandon, Oxford and Herbert. He hopes to send a message to Stanley, whose regiment is camped half a mile from Richard's forces.

At nine o'clock Richard decides he will not have supper and asks whether his battle garb is ready. Catesby is asked to send an officer to tell Stanley to bring his regiment to the battlefield before dawn, otherwise his son will be executed. Richard is distrustful of his allies, asking after Northumberland and Surrey. He withdraws to his tent with a heavy heart. Ratcliffe is to help him arm at midnight. Meanwhile Stanley arrives at Richmond's tent. He explains that he cannot support him openly because of the danger his son is in, but hopes that Richmond will 'be valiant, and speed well' (line 103). Before he retires to sleep Richmond prays to God for victory.

At this point the ghosts of Richard's victims appear onstage. They urge Richard to despair and die, but predict that Richmond will 'live and flourish' (line 139). Richard wakes out of his dream startled, afflicted by his conscience. He feels isolated and afraid. Ratcliffe accompanies him when he goes to eavesdrop on his troops. He still fears mutiny. By way of contrast, Richmond has had pleasant dreams, and his soul is 'jocund' (line 233). At four o'clock in the morning he makes an oration to his soldiers. He declares that God is on his side and reminds the men that they are fighting to 'free your children from the sword' (line 262). Richard continues to feel uneasy as he prepares his battle plan. But he sets out bravely. His oration to his army is rousing. He denigrates his opponents and urges his men to 'whip these stragglers o'er the seas again' (line 328). As the battle begins Richard learns that Stanley has deserted him. There is no time to execute his son George.

> This is a scene of contrasts. Shakespeare includes realistic and supernatural elements, and throughout we are encouraged to compare Richard and Richmond because of the way in which the dramatist structures the scene, moving from one army to the other. The realism comes from the careful delineation of time and the meticulous plans that the two leaders make. It quickly becomes apparent that Richmond is in the ascendant. His supporters are in good spirits, he sleeps well and he is convinced that the weather and his dreams are good omens. Meanwhile Richard is suspicious and ill at ease, even before his nightmare. Some critics have suggested that the villain reaches his nadir before the battle has begun, that he becomes a victim of his conscience, and that he is, in a very real sense, destroyed before he is physically dead. He nonetheless shows flashes of his old spirit and daring, as his vigorous oration to his soldiers demonstrates. If we compare this speech with Richmond's oration, it is clear that we are supposed to side with the Welshman. Richmond speaks in general terms, making much of the fact that it is God's will that he should overthrow a tyrant. He is not interested in personal gain. Significantly, Richard makes no mention of the Lord in his much more personal and colourful speech.
>
> It is difficult – even at this late stage of the play – not to find Richard more compelling than his opponent, although we know

that he can and must not survive for much longer. There are two main reasons for this. Firstly, his audacious devilry remains mesmerising. Just before his oration he says recklessly, 'Let us to it pell-mell – / If not to Heaven, then hand in hand to hell!' (lines 313–14). Here he seems to reconfirm the evil choice he made in Act I Scene 1, when he said he was 'determined' to prove a villain. Richard ultimately has the courage of his wicked convictions. These words have a particularly shocking impact because we have just witnessed Richard at his lowest point. This is the second aspect of the scene that makes the usurper fascinating; Shakespeare has developed the protagonist's character in an intriguing way in Act V Scene 3. The nightmare leads Richard to delve into his conscience and for a moment he is paralysed. He sees himself from new angles, almost as if he has multiple personalities. His panic is understandable. We may not sympathise with him, but we still feel more drawn to the protagonist than to Richmond, whose speeches are at all times calm, ceremonial and impersonal, as befits his symbolic function in the play. Richmond may be the saviour of England, but there is something heroic about Richard's resolution at the end of this scene.

The ghosts of Richard's victims, who appear in the order in which they were killed, link the past, present and future of England. Like the lamentation scenes, this parade is a solemn ritual, which starkly highlights the differences between the two leaders. The repetitive phrasing adds to the power of the ghosts' pronouncements. The ghosts are a prophetic **chorus** who announce Richard's doom. This seems appropriate. It also seems fair and **ironic** that the master ironist, so adept at using words to persuade others, should be shaken by the words of the victims he despised and mocked. The ghosts' approval of Richmond confirms our belief that the new king must be viewed as England's saviour. With his accession, these souls can rest in peace. God and the good angels will have won. For an extended commentary on part of this scene see Text 3 in Textual Analysis.

1 **Bosworth** Market Bosworth, a small town ten miles west of Leicester. The Battle of Bosworth took place in a field two miles south of the town

51 **beaver** face-guard on a helmet, which could be moved up and down

71 **cockshut time** dusk

91 **mortal-staring** able to kill with a look; another reference to the basilisk

306 **Dickon** a contemptuous reference to Richard, using a diminutive form of his name

SCENE 4   Richard fights bravely in battle

Catesby calls to Norfolk for assistance on the battlefield. Richard's horse has been killed, but the king seeks Richmond on foot. He refuses to give up.

> Our last glimpse of Richard confirms the protagonist's heroism. He has disposed of five soldiers who have acted as decoys, and still seeks his enemy Richmond when the situation looks hopeless. His last moments are violent but determined. It seems appropriate that the opportunistic **Machiavel** says he has 'set my life upon a cast, / And I will stand the hazard of the die' (lines 9–10). Instead of repenting his sins in a final **soliloquy** he will die in action.

9–10 **set my life upon a cast ... stand the hazard of the die** a gambling **metaphor**, referring to the roll of the dice

11 **six Richmonds** it was accepted practice to dress several soldiers like the king in order to confuse the enemy. The fact that he has disposed of so many impostors without reaching the real usurper is **ironic**, but it shows Richard's ferocious bravery and determination

SCENE 5   Richard is slain in battle and Richmond accepts the crown

Stanley presents the crown to the victorious Richmond. His son is safe in Leicester. The new king orders the burial of the noblemen who have perished in battle. He offers to pardon Richard's soldiers if they will be loyal to him. One of his first priorities is to marry Elizabeth of York, thus uniting the factions in England and putting an end to the Wars of the Roses. Richmond predicts a happy future for the realm under his heirs; as he says, 'peace lives again' (line 40).

> Richmond's emphasis on peace suggests that the wheel has come full circle in the play. Act I Scene 1 opened with Richard

announcing his intention to destroy the fragile peace; now we are presented with the man who promises 'smooth-fac'd peace, / With smiling plenty, and fair prosperous days' (lines 33–4). The conquering hero looks forward rather than backwards. He will unite the houses of Lancaster and York and he and Elizabeth will produce heirs who will 'Enrich the time to come' (line 33). It is clear from this final speech, which sounds like a prayer, that the mad bloodshed of the past is over. After watching Richard's vicious career it is impossible not to feel gladdened by Richmond's dignified and measured words. Order has been restored. The new sovereign has an impersonal and positive vision of England that his egotistical predecessor could never even begin to comprehend. The country is undoubtedly safe in Richmond's hands. No wonder the play closes with a resounding 'Amen'. The religious tone of the final line is intended to provide a strong sense of **closure**

19 **white rose and the red** the Yorkists used the white rose as an emblem, while the Lancastrians chose the red rose

20 **conjunction** marriage

PART THREE

CRITICAL APPROACHES

CHARACTERISATION

RICHARD III

THE SHOWMAN

Richard is appealing because he is an expert actor and trickster. During his rise to power in Acts I–III he is always in charge of himself, and acutely aware of how to play every scene to his advantage. His hypocrisy and deception are daring and breathtaking. Scornful of women, Richard is nonetheless a successful wooer. He is equally adept at playing the concerned family man, taking in his brother Clarence and then his nephews, who are convinced that he is their 'good uncle Gloucester' (II.2.20). Richard also finds it useful to take on the role of unworldly innocent, first when he carps about the queen's kindred in Act I Scene 3, and then, with wonderful élan, in Act III Scene 7 when he takes the crown. An integral part of his strategy on these occasions is to establish himself on the moral high ground as a pious and peace-loving man. But Richard is not merely skilled at fitting the role to the occasion. He has the canny ability to switch between one role and another with an alacrity that catches others off balance. This is how he manipulates, bewilders and destroys Hastings in Act III Scene 4. He begins the scene in a relaxed and jovial mood, becoming tyrannical at exactly the right moment. His acting ability is one of the most significant sources of Richard's power.

We are also drawn to Richard because he has such high spirits. He is bustling with intellectual energy and confidence for the first three acts, revelling in his devilry. It is hard to resist his gleeful enjoyment because he draws us in with his **soliloquies** and **asides**. He is also fearless, witty and **ironic**, all traits designed to win over the audience.

THE MACHIAVEL

The **Machiavel** was a villainous stock character in Elizabethan and Jacobean drama, so called after the Florentine writer Niccolò Machiavelli

(1469–1527), author of *The Prince* (written 1513), a book of political advice to rulers that recommended the need under certain circumstances to lie to the populace for their own good and to preserve power. The Machiavel was almost synonymous with the devil in English literature at this period. The Elizabethan audience would have expected stage Machiavels to behave in certain ways; they would be practised and manipulative liars, cruel opportunists who delighted in their own evil. Richard shares all these traits. Shakespeare also endows him with a number of other Machiavellian qualities. Richard is supremely individualistic, a deliberate deceiver and dissembler, who chooses to operate outside the accepted moral and religious codes of the society in which he lives. But unlike a number of malcontent or bastard upstart Machiavels in the drama of the period (Iago, *Othello*; Edmund, *King Lear*; Bosola, *The Duchess of Malfi*; Flamineo, *The White Devil*), Richard is of noble birth, and he sneers at those he considers parvenus. He is not portrayed as a product of the political climate of the age, in which old feudal ideas were being questioned. Indeed, if anything, Richard attempts to rule like a medieval tyrant, murdering everyone who stands in his way with an alarming – even reckless – brutality, which ultimately brings about his ruin. Once he has achieved the crown Richard's Machiavellian qualities are superseded by despotism and he is no longer the astute political animal we saw in the first three acts. Thus he is much more – or less – than a stage Machiavel. We need to consider another theatrical model that Shakespeare drew on when he was drawing Richard's character.

THE VICE

The **Vice** continued to be a popular character during the period when Shakespeare was writing. The Vice had its origins in the morality plays of the fifteenth and sixteenth centuries, where medieval devils, who tempted mankind, were repulsive and dangerous, but also comic. Like the stage Machiavel, the Vice had a number of stock characteristics. A solitary and amoral figure, he would be scornful of humanity, sexually and morally dubious, and a great boaster. He would draw his audiences in by addressing them directly and his speeches would be full of oaths and proverbs. He could also be witty and self-consciously theatrical. Shakespeare clearly conceives of his Richard fulfilling a number of the

Vice's functions, and the grim comedy of much of the play is similar to the tone of many of the earlier **allegorical** dramas. Like the Vice, Richard is evil incarnate, doomed to be defeated by the forces of good. The Vice, however, was not a representation of Satan, while Richard is clearly portrayed as being the devil. On a number of occasions he is cursed as 'hell's black intelligencer' (IV.4.71), suggesting that Shakespeare wishes us to see him as a truly horrific and terrifying figure. This brings us to a consideration of the religious connotations of the Tudor myth.

GOD'S SCOURGE

According to a number of Tudor historians, who sought to promote the idea of the Tudors as saviours of the realm and authors of peace and prosperity, the Wars of the Roses and the defeat of the house of York were the result of the deposition of Richard II. People were to understand that England had to suffer a period of bloody civil strife to expiate the sin of usurping God's anointed deputy. Richard III is thus the final punishment, God's scourge, sent to chastise a sinful nation. This myth was a means by which Tudor historians – many of whom conceived of history as serving moral lessons – could bolster support for the current regime and explain such a destructive period in the nation's affairs.

It is clear that Shakespeare intended his audience to understand that Richard III was part of a pattern of sin and retribution. Throughout the play the characters are forced to acknowledge their own involvement in bloody deeds. Although Richard is obviously the most accomplished villain onstage, he is not the only character with blood on his hands. In Act I Scene 3 when Margaret makes her first appearance, a number of violent deaths that have occurred during the Wars of the Roses are alluded to. We come to realise that Richard exists in a corrupt and disordered world, where murder for personal gain has become commonplace. This fact does not make Richard's evil any less shocking or abhorrent: he is a homicidal, misanthropic, amoral monster who must be destroyed, regardless of whether or not his adversaries are guilty.

THE TRAGIC ANTI-HERO?

During the period in which Shakespeare was writing there was a vogue for enigmatic or tyrannical criminals who took centre stage – Tamburlaine, Faustus and Barabas from Marlowe's work, and

Hieronimo in the early **revenge tragedy** *The Spanish Tragedy*, are all good examples of the anti-hero. Each male protagonist dominates the play in which he appears, just as Richard dominates this play. When it comes to the denouement, however, Shakespeare has a problem on his hands. In the first three acts he has established a particularly compelling villain. Richard has delighted us with his displays of exuberant and insouciant daring. We know he is bad, but he is fun to watch. Because of the theatrical models he is based on, we know he must perish. But will we not regret the demise of this wicked dynamo?

Shakespeare has to persuade us to distance ourselves from Richard. A study of his characterisation in the last two acts of the play suggests a diminishment in the villain's powers. Some would argue that Richard gradually becomes less magnetic. There is certainly a change in Act IV, when the brutal king's rage is real and not feigned (see Act IV Scene 4 when he temporarily loses control, and his temper). Self-doubt creeps in, and he starts to seem more introspective, wondering about his fate. We understand that Richard is now having to react to events, rather than always controlling them. In this scene he seems stuck. He finds that he cannot talk down his mother and Elizabeth, and the arguments he uses to try to gain Elizabeth's approval for a match with her daughter sound hollow. We heard them before when he wooed Anne. Now his methods of persuasion fail him. As his wit deserts him and he becomes more tyrannical, Richard seems weaker and less attractive. However, it is also possible to argue that while Richard becomes less sympathetic, he is no less interesting. In some ways his stature as daring anti-hero seems to be reaffirmed after his nightmare on Bosworth field. This is Richard's lowest point, but surely, for the modern audience, interested in the psychology and motivation of characters, his fraught **soliloquy** renders him more compelling? And he displays courage on the battlefield, reminding us that his reputation as a great soldier is well deserved. His reckless choice to remain a villain and go to hell may confirm his evil nature, but it is difficult not to feel the same admiration for Richard that Catesby expresses when he says the king 'enacts more wonders than a man' (V.4.2). There has always been something superhuman about his power. At the moment of his death the anti-hero does not waver. Thus Richard proves that he has successfully fulfilled his mission to 'prove a villain' (I.1.30). Can we applaud him for his stoicism?

This point brings us to the question of **tragedy**. What qualities of the tragic hero does Shakespeare endow his historical monster with? According to Aristotle, tragedy should provoke two emotions in the audience: terror and pity. Watching Richard, it is certainly easy to be horror-struck. But can we pity the anti-hero? Probably not. Richard is not, ultimately, a true tragic hero because he does not suffer for his sins as the other great Shakespearean tragedians suffer. Othello and Lear, for example, undergo extreme torment, and learn the truth about themselves before they meet tragic ends. Richard knows himself only too well. He is not a good man who makes a fatal error of judgement. He is a self-confessed villain. He learns nothing, and comes to no new understanding about himself, the nature of humanity, or the world in which he lives. He dies unrepentant. Unlike Lear and Othello, Richard does not seem to have a fatal character flaw either. He is brought down by characters more virtuous than himself, and it is possible to argue that although pride is one of Richard's sins, his whole character is faulty. He does not have any positive characteristics that suggest that the world will be a sorrier place without him. Indeed, the play suggests the opposite is true. Without Richard, England will be a saner and safer place. We admire Othello and Lear for many reasons. These two heroes have characteristics of greatness, and they inspire love in other virtuous characters. Richard can only be admired for his performance, not for his essence. Justly, no one loves him.

RICHARD'S FAMILY

EDWARD IV
We see little evidence of Edward as 'glorious ... son of York' (I.1.2) in this play. He is an ailing man from the first scene in which he appears, and his ill health is a cause for concern from Act I Scene 1 onwards. Nonetheless, we recognise that he has good intentions when he tries to reconcile the factions at his court. Although he is both husband and father, as well as ruler, we do not see Edward in these roles. That Elizabeth cares for him we know; she frets about him in Act I and later mourns him sincerely, suggesting that this marriage is a happier affair than Anne's wretched match with Richard. The historical focus of the play means that the domestic sphere is significantly less important than

the political arena. And it is in the latter where Edward is – perhaps – found wanting. The Elizabethan audience would have known that England had enjoyed a period of peace and prosperity under his rule, but in *Richard III* we see the consequences of Edward's poor judgement and ill fortune. There are two specific examples which suggest that he was not the perfect ruler. Firstly, he is responsible for the advancement of his wife's relatives, which has caused dissent. Secondly, even though Shakespeare makes it plain that Richard must take the lion's share of the blame for Clarence's death, Edward signed a death warrant. The play does not suggest that the king has done these things with evil intent, but he has not considered the consequences of his actions closely enough, and after his death his lack of foresight plunges the realm – and his family – into crisis. Edward has one powerful speech, and, significantly, it is delivered when it is too late. He expresses deep regret when Clarence dies, questioning his advisers and asking why they did not intervene to save his younger brother. Like so many of the characters in this play, Edward is wise after the event. And as on so many occasions, Richard is able to triumph because weak men remain silent. This pattern continues throughout the play. As for bad luck, Edward's misfortune is to die early, before his son has reached his majority. Shakespeare suggests that he dies because of ill health, but even here Richard seems to have played a part. Edward collapses immediately after he learns Clarence is dead, and never recovers. This is not simply a personal tragedy for his family. Because Edward is king, the whole realm is affected, and as the citizens remind us, 'Woe to that land that's govern'd by a child' (II.3.11).

There is one other aspect of his characterisation that makes us doubt Edward as a ruler: his sexuality. He shares a mistress with his friend Hastings, and the legitimacy of his marriage can be questioned. Sexual incontinence becomes an important issue when Richard makes his bid for the crown. He makes much of female frailty, but perhaps the modern audience will recognise that Edward was not perhaps a good role model, even if Richard's claims are as outrageous here as they are elsewhere.

CLARENCE
Shakespeare's presentation of Clarence does not focus closely on a number of important historical facts, most significantly his treacherous

plots against his brother Edward. He is characterised as an essentially benign and innocent man, who holds his brothers in high esteem. It does not serve the dramatist's purpose to look too closely at the reasons for his imprisonment; Shakespeare is more interested in the theme of conscience and in the consequences of Clarence's death. However, like his brothers, Clarence has played his bloody part in the Wars of the Roses, and he acknowledges and expresses remorse for some of his actions. This is the most important feature of Clarence's characterisation. His regret makes Clarence more worthy than his treacherous younger sibling, and his murder is more affecting as a result. Clarence is Richard's first male victim, and the fact that Richard begins his murderous career in this play with fratricide demonstrates the extent of his evil. Like Edward, Clarence leaves behind vulnerable children, whose lives are blasted when he is gone. Richard's allusions to Clarence's offspring show how children, as well as men and women, are forced to live in fear when wickedness triumphs.

PRINCE EDWARD & DUKE RICHARD OF YORK

Unlike their father and uncle Clarence, the young princes are entirely innocent of any crime. They are Richard's most pathetic victims. Both boys are delineated carefully by the dramatist, who needs to establish them as distinct and engaging personalities if their deaths are to be truly affecting. Prince Edward is a dignified child, who shows his patriotism and valour when he declares that he hopes to recover Britain's French territories when he is king. We recognise that this aim is worthy of respect. Edward's feelings of foreboding about the Tower suggest both sensitivity and wisdom. Shakespeare intends us to see that the country is losing a promising sovereign when Edward is murdered. By way of contrast, the Duke of York is a more lively boy, who enjoys jests and wordplay. He mocks Richard and his brother, revealing a sharp intelligence. His wittiness makes York attractive. Appropriately, Tyrrel's eloquent epitaph (IV.3.1–22) for the 'gentle' lads focuses on their pious beauty. Their premature, ugly deaths will chill the audience. After these murders it is very difficult to respond positively to Richard.

THE DUCHESS OF YORK

Richard's mother is a minor figure, but her rejection of her youngest son is important. She reminds us that Richard has been a source of worry to her, a dreadful prodigy, from the moment that he was born. Her energetic curses – particularly in Act IV Scene 4 – show us how repugnant Richard is; he is so bad that even his mother cannot find a good word to say about him. Richard's impatience with and contempt for her show his inhuman lack of filial feeling. As grieving mother and grandmother, the Duchess of York, like Margaret, reminds us of the destructive cycle that has gripped England during the Wars of the Roses.

ANNE

It is fitting that Richard's bride should be an isolated and weak figure, who remains on the sidelines after the first scene in which she appears. Anne's wretched life highlights the plight of all the female characters in this play, who are helpless victims. But unlike her mother-in-law and, arguably, Elizabeth, Anne is in some senses a 'fallen' woman. She is undoubtedly hoodwinked by Richard, but since she has been the wife of Henry VI's virtuous son we suspect that she should not make the mistake of uniting herself with a man she knows is a butcher. Nonetheless, it is easy to feel sympathy for Anne, even if she makes a bad moral choice in Act I. She is utterly miserable after her second marriage and knows that her husband wishes her dead. Like so many of Richard's victims, she is wise after the event, and suffers terribly. Anne provides us with one important piece of information about Richard: he sleeps badly and is wakened by 'timorous dreams' (IV.1.84). Even before we see him in the aftermath of his nightmare on Bosworth field, we know that Richard's conscience will catch up with him. Anne's most significant role is to show us Richard the seducer. The persuasive but perverse charm he displays in Act I Scene 2 is a key to his success.

ALLIES

BUCKINGHAM

Buckingham – a very powerful nobleman – is Richard's most important ally. He is an able politician; discreet and apparently non-committal in the first scene in which he appears, he soon joins forces with Gloucester, encouraged by the belief that he will prosper under the usurper. But in spite of being 'deep-revolving, witty' (IV.2.42) and a fine rhetorician, he makes mistakes. He would have done well to heed Margaret's warnings in Act I Scene 3, but, like Richard, his ambition is overweening. When he hesitates in Act IV Scene 2 he is lost. Richard sacrifices him as ruthlessly as he discards his wife and disposes of his nephews. We are not surprised by this. We saw Buckingham's complacent hypocrisy in Act III Scene 5 when he helped Richard in his quest for the throne, and know he must be punished. Like earlier victims Clarence and Hastings, he realises too late that he cannot trust Richard. He wisely chooses to flee, but in spite of his rebellion Buckingham is unlucky. He is captured and put to death. We will not mourn his passing, recognising his folly in making a pact with the devil.

CATESBY

Unlike Buckingham, who can be both smooth and sophisticated in his villainy, Catesby is direct. He plays an important role in bringing down Hastings. He also plays his part in Act III Scene 7, assisting Buckingham as he urges Gloucester to accept the crown. Thereafter his role is less significant, although he is a useful messenger and commentator, keeping us informed about Richard's state of mind and the progress of the enemy. Catesby remains loyal to his master on the battlefield, and offers us a view of Richard as brave soldier in Act V Scene 4. It seems appropriate that this double-dealing pragmatist should be the last man to speak to the demon king before he dies.

RATCLIFFE

Ratcliffe is a minor character but, like Catesby, he is a useful henchman. His black humour in Act III Scene 4 mirrors Richard's. Ratcliffe is part brutal enforcer, part messenger. He is the one who gets his hands dirty in Richard's service, playing key roles in the executions of Hastings, Rivers, Grey and Vaughan. He too remains loyal to his master until he dies.

TYRREL

We are told that Tyrrel, who is indirectly responsible for the deaths of the princes in the Tower (he organises the murders), is a 'discontented gentleman' with a 'haughty spirit' who can be corrupted by gold and tempted to 'anything' (IV.2.36–9). Thus, like Buckingham, Tyrrel is a proud and amoral man, motivated by personal gain. But, like the other murderers hired by Richard, he seems to be struck by his conscience when the heinous deed is done, commenting soberly that he has arranged 'The most arch deed of piteous massacre / That ever yet this land was guilty of' (IV.3.2–3). These are powerful phrases and we know that Tyrrel will suffer the same fate as the others who have made a pact with the devil: he is damned.

ADVERSARIES

HASTINGS

A foolish man, Hastings believes that he can choose not to support Richard and keep his head. Unlike Richard's other adversaries, he does not curse or distrust the Protector, but he does not have the political wit to protect himself (unlike Stanley). He is blind and complacent, believing that Richard 'loves me well' (III.4.14) up to the moment he is accused of treason. Like Anne, he chooses to misinterpret the usurper's character and words, and pays the price with his life; like Buckingham, Hastings should have heeded the warnings offered to him. It is **ironic** that the most subtle and naïve male victims in the play should share the same fate because they fail to say what Richard wants to hear.

MARGARET

Ironically Richard's fiercest critic shares some of her enemy's characteristics. Margaret is a forceful rhetorician, skilled at using her tongue to destroy those she despises. She is not cowed by her adversaries. She is a vigorous and arresting woman, in spite of her age and lack of political power. Like Richard, she is essentially a lone figure, whose crimes ultimately render her unsympathetic, even if we recognise her wisdom as prophetess. Margaret's bloody-minded vituperation is unique in the play. Her vengeful quality is theatrically compelling, even though she has no **soliloquies** and is essentially a static commentator, part Greek Fury, part **chorus**. Margaret may be one-dimensional in her bitter gloating, we may even feel, as some critics do, that she is lifeless, but she becomes an unlikely source of inspiration for the other female characters, who gradually become skilful detractors themselves. Margaret's most important role is to remind the audience of the destructive cycles of history. She drives home the idea that the villain must face a reckoning, just as she has. By making her so unattractive, Shakespeare is recalling the horrors of the Wars of the Roses, which will come to an end with Richmond's accession. We will be glad when this bitter Lancastrian is finally silent, just as we are meant to rejoice when the 'bottled spider' is killed. The form of justice Margaret represents is pitiless and warped.

ELIZABETH

Elizabeth becomes more intriguing as the play progresses. **Ironically** her role becomes more significant when she is no longer queen and is seemingly powerless. She knows that she cannot trust her brother-in-law, while many noblemen still seem to believe that Richard is honest and worthy, and her fears prove accurate. Thus we are given a hint early on that Elizabeth might become a force to be reckoned with. However, for much of the first four acts she is a passive and innocent victim, unable to make any choices that will affect the lives of her kindred in a positive way. She is forced to flee to sanctuary and to give up her young sons, who are brutally murdered. Having bewailed their fates, Elizabeth then gains enough strength to confront Richard in one of the longest scenes in the play, where she causes him a good deal of trouble and discomfort before seeming to capitulate to his demand that she should allow him to marry her eldest daughter. At the moment when it looks as if she has lost everything, she turns the tables on Richard. Elizabeth reneges on her promise and Richmond is offered the girl. We are also informed that Elizabeth has managed to save her remaining son by sending him abroad. It seems fitting that the mother of the first Tudor queen should prove, ultimately, to be a courageous survivor.

THE QUEEN'S KINDRED

Shakespeare does not provide detailed portraits of Elizabeth's family, Dorset, Rivers and Grey. Her brother, Rivers, and son from her first marriage, Grey, are put to death by Richard. Dorset survives, hastily packed off abroad, where he joins forces with Richmond, so that he does not suffer the same fate as his sibling. In spite of Richard's complaint that Elizabeth's kindred are upstarts with too much influence at court, we must see them as innocent victims. They do not say or do anything to merit suspicion. In the only scene in which they appear as a family group – Act I Scene 3 – Queen Elizabeth's kindred seem to be a close-knit clan. Her brother defends her against Richard's accusations and insults, while her sons attempt to comfort Elizabeth. All three show some spirit when dealing with their adversary Richard, particularly Rivers. In Act III Scene 3 we see Rivers and Grey stoical in the face of death. They retain their dignity, recognising their folly in not listening to Margaret's warnings. Like Clarence, they call on God to be 'satisfied ... with our true blood' (line 22) and not wreak further vengeance on the family. These may be vain hopes, but they are worthy sentiments.

STANLEY

Stanley shares some of Buckingham's traits. He is a powerful nobleman who proves to be an able politician. But, unlike Buckingham, he does not suspend his judgement and never makes the mistake of trusting Richard. He survives because he is cautious, and because he is able to use three of Richard's most deadly weapons against him: hypocrisy, intrigue and good timing. He appears to support Richard, never giving him overt proof of disloyalty, although the wily sovereign suspects Stanley of plotting against him. As late as the Battle of Bosworth Richard is unsure which way Stanley will jump: will he defect to Richmond or lead his troops out for the Plantagenet king? We know how brave Stanley is when he chooses to support Richmond because Richard has taken his son hostage in an effort to force his hand. Throughout the play we have been encouraged to believe that Stanley is a loyal subject of England, who has the country's best interests at heart. He is not motivated by self-interest, although he keeps a politic silence for much of Richard's bloody career. He generously warns Hastings about Richard's treachery early on. He helps Elizabeth to save Dorset, and he times his own desertion so that his son survives. Stanley gains in stature as the play progresses, and by the time he places the crown on Richmond's head in the final scene, we know that we can trust his judgement enough to view this usurpation as beneficial and just.

RICHMOND

An audience might feel justified in dismissing the conquering hero as a one-dimensional cut-out. As is the case with Margaret, there seems to be little character development during the scenes in which he appears. Nor does Richmond possess any of the characteristics that make Richard so theatrically compelling. He makes no attempt to draw us in and we are not given a glimpse of what we might consider a rounded personality. But Shakespeare does not need us to be fascinated by Richmond as a man. He is a symbol, a representative of God and the forces of good. We might even be relieved to see Richard usurped by a man whose words are devoid of **irony**. Richmond speaks in measured tones, employing religious **imagery** in a straightforward way. He is a dignified, gracious and brave soldier, and his self-confidence is justified because he is fighting to restore order and justice in a land that has been all but destroyed; he is not on an egotistical mission. Thus Richmond is a simplified hero, the polar opposite of the scheming and subtle villain he seeks to replace. For critics who see this play as a validation of the Tudor myth, which vilified Richard III, Richmond is a figure more suited to a propaganda pamphlet than the stage. But you might consider this question: is Shakespeare's portrait of the dull and pallid Richmond not rather subversive? Even as we share the characters' relief that the 'bloody dog' (V.5.2) is dead, might we not also feel regret that he has been cut down by the theatrical equivalent of a milksop?

RICHARD III & HISTORY

The Tudor historian John Hardyng believed that history should serve as 'a lanterne, to the posteritee'. It should indicate 'what waies to refuse, and what to folowe' (quoted in Lily B. Campbell's essay 'English History in the Sixteenth Century' in *Shakespeare: The Histories*, edited by Waith, 1965, p. 13). His words outline the view held by a number of **humanist** historians working at this period: history was a means by which people could be taught moral lessons. Thus one of its most important functions was to instruct. This was not a new idea; it was derived from Classical models of Greek and Roman history. According to Cicero, history 'bears witness to the passing of the ages, sheds light upon reality, gives life to recollection and guidance to human existence' (quoted in Holderness's *Shakespeare: The Histories*, 2000, p. 42). Through the careful reconstruction of the past, Renaissance historians sought to continue in this tradition. They were on a mission to understand and to evaluate the present. Lily B. Campbell says that Renaissance historians worked hard to show that history was 'a connected, unified narrative' ('English History in the Sixteenth Century', p. 17), in which cause and effect were intimately and incontrovertibly linked. History was essentially a didactic genre and, as a result, inherently political.

Clearly this approach to history suited the Tudor rulers well. It was in their interests that the reign of the last Plantagenet king should be presented in a harsh and unflattering light, in order to justify the usurpation of the throne by Henry VII. The 'bloody dog' Richard had to be shown to be a cruel tyrant, whose actions deserved punishment not simply by his fellow men, but also by God. During the Renaissance the moral dimension of history was related to Christian beliefs, specifically the prevailing Elizabethan conception of the world order, which had not changed significantly since the medieval period (although contemporary critics and historians would argue that it was being questioned during the late sixteenth century). According to Tillyard, the Elizabethans believed that 'the universe was a unity, in which everything had its place, and it was the perfect work of God' ('The Elizabethan World Order' in Waith, ed., *Shakespeare: The Histories*, p. 33). When unity was threatened, God intervened to punish those who sought to undermine or destroy His creation. Linked to the idea of 'degree' and the 'chain of being' – God's regulation of His creatures – was the concept of the divine right of kings, another tenet that dated back to the medieval period. Those who subscribed to this belief held that it was a sin to revolt against God's anointed deputy on earth. Tudor historians, then, found themselves confronted by a thorny paradox: Richmond, the usurper, who was, on the surface, as great a villain as the man he defeated, had to be presented as a hero. They got round the problem by presenting the Wars of the Roses as a terrible and destructive cycle, the dreadful outcome of the usurpation of Richard II. Thus Richard III becomes God's scourge, sent by the Almighty to punish the nation for its crimes. England, having brought evil on itself by allowing Richard II to be overthrown, had to suffer before it was cleansed by the Tudor dynasty.

The historical sources that Shakespeare turned to when he was preparing to write *Richard III* presented similar damning versions of the demon king's reign. The most important sources were Sir Thomas

More's *History of King Richard the thirde* and the chronicles of Hall and Holinshed. More's history is unfinished, dealing only with Gloucester's rise to power, but it presents a masterly portrait of a scheming villain. It is psychologically compelling, and full of arresting descriptions and assessments of Richard's bad character. Critics have argued that Shakespeare was heavily indebted to More, and that the second half of *Richard III* is less powerful than the first because the dramatist did not have More to rely on when it came to details of Richard's reign. Hall and Holinshed were both influenced by More, and by the first humanist historian to write a history of England that covered a lengthy period of time, the Italian Polydore Vergil. Vergil's *Urbinatis Anglicae Historiae* (1534) includes summaries of personal characters, a new feature of Renaissance historical writing. Hall's chronicles, covering the reigns of eight English kings, from Henry IV to Henry VIII, appeared in 1548, while Holinshed's work was first published in 1577. Shakespeare would have been familiar with the revised edition of Holinshed that appeared in 1587. All of these histories are morality tales. If he had wanted to work from unbiased sources, Shakespeare would have found it impossible to locate any.

LITERARY MODELS & SOURCES

Shakespeare was indebted to dramatists and poets as well as historians. At the time that he was writing, playwrights did not view their art as a separate genre which had nothing in common with the work of historians. They believed, like historians, that they produced works which were capable of telling moral truths. Thomas Heywood defended the ideological purposes of his craft in *An Apology for Actors* in 1612 (the following extract is taken from Holderness's *Shakespeare: The Histories*, 2000, p. 48):

> playes haue made the ignorant more apprehensiue, taught the vnlearned the knowledge of many famous histories, instructed such as cannot reade in the discovery of all our *English* Chronicles.

History plays, then, served a useful educational purpose. Watching them, the audience would learn useful lessons about the consequences of good and evil behaviour.

Heywood may have been writing long after the medieval mystery and morality plays had been replaced by more sophisticated dramatic forms, but his words remind us of the religious origins and didactic functions of early English drama. Shakespeare's Richard III, who is part morality **Vice** (see Characterisation), is not entirely divorced from his dramatic predecessors. Shakespeare's presentation of the last Plantagenet's reign is inspired by other literary sources too, one of the most important being *A Mirror for Magistrates*, a series of poems that includes coverage of a number of events which occurred during Richard's career. Published between 1559 and 1587, these verse monologues are 'spoken' by English statesmen and princes who have suffered misfortunes in their public lives. Like Tudor history and history plays, the poems were written with a moral purpose to teach rulers and their subjects the consequences of immoral and violent actions. Buckingham and Clarence both 'speak' in the *Mirror*, and it is likely that Shakespeare's presentation of their characters owes something to this ambitious, ethical work.

History and **tragedy**, which were not seen as separate genres during the Elizabethan period, were heavily influenced by Classical drama. In *Richard III* there are several elements that derive from Senecan tragedy: Richard's tyranny and stoicism, his desire for revenge and the presentation of the women as a lamenting and static **chorus**. The sensational and supernatural elements in the play – the ghosts, the bloody murders that occur offstage – and the formal rhetoric are also inspired by Classical, heroic drama.

There were contemporary dramatic works that would have helped Shakespeare create his portrait of the villain-hero too. Thomas Kyd's *Spanish Tragedy* (*c.*1589) paved the way for dramatists who wished to present bloody tales of amoral outsiders in **revenge tragedies**, and we must not underestimate Christopher Marlowe's unorthodox influence. An atheist, Marlowe wrote two plays in which murderous, gleeful and individualistic brutes are presented as triumphant winners: *Tamburlaine the Great* (1587) and *The Jew of Malta* (*c.*1589). In *Tamburlaine* in particular, the dramatist appears to undermine ideas about Elizabethan absolutism and the role of providence in human affairs. *The Jew of Malta* opens with a speech by **Machiavel**, a character Richard of Gloucester links himself to in *3 Henry VI* when he says he possesses the cunning to 'set the murderous Machiavel to school' (III.2.193). In the same play he utters these lines:

> I have no brother, I am like no brother;
> And this word 'love', which greybeards call divine,
> Be resident in men like one another,
> And not in me: I am myself alone. (V.6.80–3)

The cool, egotistical iconoclasm of these lines is distinctly Marlovian, and gives a flavour of what we see enacted in *Richard III*. Like the Machiavel, Gloucester uses any means necessary to achieve his aims. (For further comments about Richard as Machiavel, see Characterisation.)

STRUCTURE

There are a variety of points to be made about the structure of *Richard III*. Firstly, it differs from the *Henry VI* plays, which are episodic. Although they focus on the reign of a particular monarch, they are not by any means 'one man' plays, as *Richard III* undoubtedly is. For the first time in his writing career Shakespeare allows one character to dominate the proceedings from the outset. Many would argue that this is a structural weakness. Because Richard is so vital, the other characters can seem flat, and when Richard's powers begin to wane, so, some would say, does our interest. However, Shakespeare has a number of dramatic weapons in his armoury which help to offset this fault, if indeed it is a fault.

Although there is no **sub-plot** to divert our attention away from Richard's bloody progress, the play is nevertheless balanced. Scenes are mirrored so that an impression of symmetry is achieved. For example, there are two wooing scenes (of Anne and Elizabeth), two scenes in which blind and complacent advisers meet sticky ends (Hastings and Buckingham), two key scenes in which Margaret makes and then confirms the justice of her prophecies and two 'dream' scenes (Clarence's and Richard's). The final dream sequence is vividly realised onstage when the ghosts of Richard's victims appear on Bosworth field. All the early examples of mirroring lead up to this telling episode, which is powerful because it is so ritualistic. The purpose of this symmetry is to show the inevitability of Richard's fall; he is stuck in a destructive cycle, from which he cannot escape. The wheel of fortune will drag him down, regardless of his actions. The cyclical movement of the play is emphasised by the repetition of key words and phrases. When he kills Richard on the battlefield Richmond declares that 'the bloody dog is dead' (V.5.2), echoing words that have been used to describe the villain throughout the play.

But the balanced structure of the play also suggests that Richard actively makes the wrong choices. He chooses to repeat his crimes, and he learns nothing in the process. Even when his conscience is awakened, he does not express regret. Thus he is damned. The structure of the play emphasises his evil. He encounters a series of victims, and sinks lower with every murder he commits. By the time he has the young princes stifled in the Tower, it is absolutely clear that Richard is unremittingly evil. Several critics see this heinous act as the turning point in the play. Up to Act IV Richard's victims have all been figures who are tainted by guilt themselves; thus we might feel that they deserve punishment, even if we cannot condone the villain's actions. Even Anne is morally suspect. Colluding with her seducer, she suspends her judgement in a moment of weakness and is lost. The princes, however, are innocent children. Their deaths show us that we are in a deeply corrupt world that needs cleansing. Shakespeare's use of mirroring ultimately distances us from the bustling villain, who becomes more repugnant as his tyranny grows. The repetition of prophecies and ritualistic lamentations also helps to alienate us and **foreshadow** the outcome of the play.

In the second half of the play Shakespeare seems intent on exploring the limitations of Richard's evil. The **irony** that is a strong feature of Richard's characterisation is turned against him in Acts IV–V, as the women he despises fight back, Stanley moves towards active rebellion and Richmond's star begins to rise. Richard's sangfroid deserts him when he fails to win Buckingham's support for the murder of the princes, and the ironic reversal of fortunes begins. The supreme manipulator finds himself reacting to others. He resorts to spying on his soldiers, and finds that his conscience will not lie dormant. He even begins to wonder about the value of prophecy, something he dismissed out of hand in his first sneering encounter with Margaret. Some would argue that the structure of the play demonstrates the decline of Richard's intellect as well as his fortunes. The limitations of despotism and atheism are revealed when Richmond, God's champion, defeats him in Act V.

Richard III is not simply a play of two phases: rise and fall. Four movements, resembling those of a Classical **tragedy**, can be identified. The introduction (**protasis**) begins in Act I Scene 1, continuing until Act I Scene 4. In Act II the plot becomes more complicated when Edward dies (**epitasis**). The action reaches a peak and Richard's fortunes begin to turn between Act III Scene 7 and Act IV Scene 4 (**catastasis**). Finally, the denouement (**catastrophe**) brings the play to a close in Act V. Shakespeare deliberately telescopes time in the play in order to make Richard's rise and fall more dramatically compelling. In reality, the events that we see took place over quite a long period of time, between 1478 (the year of Clarence's death) and 1485. The dramatist also adapts and manipulates the events of history freely in order to bring the themes he wishes to explore into sharp focus, and to ensure that we understand the central message that the villain is trapped and doomed because he is part of a vicious cycle.

What is perhaps missing in Richard III is comic relief. The structure may resemble that of tragedy, but the audience is not really allowed to experience any significant light moments away from the villain-hero. Richard is the primary source of humour in the play, and his is a black and knowing humour which becomes increasingly repellent. Clarence's murderers and Richard's henchmen are infected by their master's ironical brutalism, but their presence increases anxiety. The second half of the play is appropriately devoid of humour. Tyrrel's sober epitaph for the princes contrasts vividly with the earlier debate between Clarence and his murderers, and the scene in which Richard woos Elizabeth shows that the witty villain has lost his touch. Arguably, Richard's loss of his sense of humour is another means by which Shakespeare can distance his audience. The humour in the play is, as Janis Lull, editor of the recent New Cambridge edition of Richard III, suggests, 'very unSenecan'. It is perhaps partly derived from the sources the dramatist used. More's history of Richard has a distinctly ironical tone, while the **Vice** of medieval drama was essentially a comic figure. Marlowe's presentation of violence and his villain-heroes is also characterised by the kind of grim humour we find in Richard III.

Shakespeare's style in this early history play shows his reliance on Classical models. *Richard III* is full of rhetorical devices found in Senecan tragedy. The Elizabethans admired skilful rhetoricians, and the dramatist would have been taught at school how to write and speak using the tropes of rhetoric – **metaphor, allegory, irony, hyperbole, synecdoche** and **metonymy** – effectively. The stylised verbal patterning of the lamentation scenes is one obvious example of Shakespeare's use of rhetoric in *Richard III*. The use of **anaphora** and **epistrophe** has a powerful impact on the audience:

> MARGARET: I had an Edward, till a Richard kill'd him;
> I had a husband, till a Richard kill'd him:
> Thou hadst an Edward, till a Richard kill'd him;
> Thou hadst a Richard, till a Richard kill'd him.
>
> DUCHESS: I had a Richard too, and thou didst kill him;
> I had a Rutland too: thou holp'st to kill him.
>
> MARGARET: Thou hadst a Clarence too, and Richard kill'd him. (IV.4.40–6)

In spite of the contrived and artificial nature of these lines, the accusations the women hurl at each other are made more powerful by the force of repetition.

There are other examples of rhetoric. When they are onstage together the women declaim rather than converse, offering a litany of their woes and cursing their enemy with a string of diabolical metaphors: 'cacodemon', 'hell-hound', 'fiend', 'devil'. Clarence's description of his dream is loaded with metaphors that add to the pathos of his predicament. In the wooing scenes, Richard and his interlocutors speak in **stichomythia**. Richard excels at rational disputation, and even the murderers have a debate before they drown Clarence. Richmond's speeches in Act V are full of **personification**, giving him a lofty, detached tone appropriate to the conquering hero: 'England hath long been mad, and scarr'd herself ... Enrich the time to come with smooth-fac'd peace, / With smiling plenty, and fair prosperous days' (V.5.23–34). When his conscience finally catches up with him, Shakespeare conveys the division in Richard's self through the use of **antithesis**.

Richard III is also fond of **double entendres, puns** and irony. In Acts I–III we see his enjoyment of wordplay in every scene in which he appears. But he is not simply a fine rhetorician. He is also a plain-spoken villain:

> RICHARD [to BUCKINGHAM]: Cousin, thou wast not wont to be so dull,
> Shall I be plain? I wish the bastards dead,
> And I would have it suddenly perform'd.
> What say'st thou now? Speak suddenly, be brief. (IV.2.17–20)

The short, clipped phrases, devoid of **imagery**, convey Richard's impatient brutalism perfectly. His speech is littered with oaths and proverbs when he is speaking in **soliloquy** or with his allies. This down-to-earth style, a notable feature of Renaissance writing, is appropriate to this bloody-minded, practical schemer, who has no truck with organised religion and mocks the formal laws and ceremonies of the world he inhabits. His ability to manipulate and parody rhetoric demonstrates the depth of his evil. Richard's actorly qualities make us deeply suspicious of his use of language in this play; essentially, he makes words meaningless when he shows off his verbal skills. Some would argue that this makes the play subversive. By the time we hear Richmond's declamations, we have learnt not to trust men who speak skilfully.

This is not to detract from Richard's power. In his opening soliloquy the villain's control of himself **foreshadows** his manipulation of others. Here he plays all the parts himself; he offers an **epilogue** on his brother's reign and then sets the scene for his own villainy, rather like a **choric** figure. Thus the speech has some of the qualities of a **prologue.** Richard describes and analyses his own character. At the end of his opening speech it becomes clear that Gloucester is already up to his neck in murderous plots, suggesting that the action of *Richard III* began before the principal character set foot on the stage. Richard is both actor and commentator, hogging the limelight from line 1 onwards.

Finally, *Richard III* is written in **blank verse,** with a number of long speeches and exchanges. This formality adds to the powerful sense of ritual that Shakespeare is often seeking to create.

There are a number of recurring images and **metaphors** that add to our understanding of *Richard III*. Appropriately, since this is a play about good and evil, there are a number of references to heaven and hell, which establish the moral context. There are a large number of images and phrases that can be linked to Christian beliefs. Henry VI is called 'that dear saint' (IV.1.69), a metaphor which encourages us to compare the dead king with his godless successor, whose piety is a sham. Judgement Day is alluded to on a number of occasions, reminding us that Richard is doomed and will face a reckoning. Appropriately, his usurper Richmond employs biblical cadences and images in his oration to his troops, and when he offers his prayer for England at the end of the play. Throughout, the religious imagery encourages us to see God's purpose being fulfilled.

The animal metaphors that are applied to Richard can also be linked to the religious themes and ideas that are explored in the play. The villain is compared with dogs, hogs, boars, spiders and toads, all of which had sinister connotations in the time that Shakespeare was writing. Dogs were thought to be not only faithful creatures, but also envious. Toads and spiders were traditionally associated with the devil, while the hog or boar was a symbol of greed and lust. The repeated use of these images adds to our negative impression of Richard, who is also characterised as an unnatural butcher. The frequent references to poison and venom consolidate the animal imagery. A number of vivid compounds add to the intensity of the insults that are hurled at Richard: 'elvish-mark'd', 'hell-hound', 'stone-hard', 'bunch-back'd'. The villain's physical deformities, which are made much of in the play, add to the impression of a grotesque being. References to food and eating suggest Richard's monstrous, animal appetite for blood and power, while descriptions of clothing remind us that Richard is self-consciously acting out a variety of roles, including that of villain. *Richard III* is a play about playing. In Act III Scene 5 Shakespeare draws our attention to this fact:

> Enter RICHARD *and* BUCKINGHAM *in rotten armour, marvellous ill-favoured.*

> RICHARD: Come, cousin, canst thou quake and change thy colour,
> Murder thy breath in middle of a word,
> And then again begin, and stop again,
> As if thou were distraught and mad with terror?

BUCKINGHAM: Tut, I can counterfeit the deep tragedian,
Speak, and look back, and pry on every side,
Tremble and start at wagging of a straw,
Intending deep suspicion. (III.5.1–8)

The complacent Buckingham clearly does not believe that he needs
acting lessons; together the 'deep tragedian' and his patron beguile the
Lord Mayor with a tour de force of stage management and counterfeit
humility. The histrionic style described in these lines is only one of the
many modes that Richard finds useful.

The images evoked to describe death add to our understanding of
Richard's crimes. The watery imagery of Clarence's dream symbolises
death, and prepares us for his drowning in the butt of malmsey. Lady
Anne's speeches in Act I Scene 2 are full of references to blood, wounds
and slaughter, even before her seducer arrives. We are told that the corpse
of Henry VI has begun to bleed again, physical proof (if any is needed)
that his murderer is on hand. The **personification** Anne employs is
repellent: 'See, see dead Henry's wounds / Open their congeal'd mouths
and bleed afresh' (I.2.55–6). The excess of 'this deluge most unnatural'
(line 61) convinces us that Richard is the epitome of evil. All the other
deaths that occur or are alluded to during the course of the play are
painful and premature. The murder of children is particularly horrible.
Margaret is 'Steep'd in the faultless blood of pretty Rutland' (I.3.178),
while her son Edward died in his youth of 'untimely violence' (I.3.201),
'stabb'd with bloody daggers' (I.3.212). The death of the princes in the
Tower is a 'tyrannous and bloody act ... ruthless butchery' (IV.3.1–5). A
clear pattern emerges: the Wars of the Roses have been a cycle of
bloodletting, which will not stop until the man with the most blood on
his hands is destroyed. When Richmond triumphs, he promises that he
has 'stopp'd' England's 'civil wounds' (V.5.40). No more blood will be
spilt.

References to the seasons and to gardens, trees and orchards help us
to understand England's plight under Richard. In the opening **soliloquy**
Richard informs us that his brother's reign is like a 'glorious summer'
(I.1.2). By way of contrast, he himself is a 'shadow in the sun' (I.1.26), an
antagonist. When Richmond unites 'the white rose and the red' (V.5.19),
the houses of York and Lancaster, the garden of England will return to

'fair prosperous days' of 'smiling plenty' (V.5.34). The natural imagery in the play reminds us of the Fall and the Garden of Eden, which is again appropriate in a play about good and evil.

THEMES

GOOD & EVIL

Richard III is a study in evil. The villain has no redeeming features, save perhaps his wit. This makes him an appealing theatrical creation. We are astounded by the wickedness presented to us, and shocked because we are amused by it. His godless mockery of piety and tradition makes Richard a particularly outrageous figure. However, in spite of the villain's power, many critics would argue that the presentation of evil in this play is crude. Richard is obviously sadistic, he dissembles effortlessly, and few are foolish enough to trust him. Again and again characters are warned about the villain's capacity for devilry. Many who fall foul of Richard are morally frail themselves. Richard's victims are, almost without exception, weak and powerless. And, arguably, the villain never really wrestles with his conscience: he is simply bad through and through. Does the lack of suspense in *Richard III* detract from the presentation of evil?

Goodness is in short supply in this play, and I would argue that it is the lack of dependable virtue that makes the play really intriguing. England has been governed by a series of guilty men and women. Margaret, Richard's sworn foe, is corrupt and self-serving. Likewise, Edward and Clarence have blood on their hands. There is little to regret when they die. The only truly 'good' characters in the play, the young princes, are consigned to the pages of history before they have proved their worth. For four acts Richard has no real adversary to stop him in his evil tracks. Richmond appears late in the play, and although we do not doubt his moral worth, his virtues are not as engaging as the villain's wickedness. Ultimately, although it may be crude, evil is more compelling than goodness in this play. Was it Shakespeare's intention that we should feel this way when the curtain comes down on Act V?

There is one other point to be made about the presentation of evil in this play. Some critics have suggested that Richard is a ritual scapegoat, who is made evil by the corrupt society he has grown up in. If you subscribe to this reading of the text, then it is possible – to an extent – to exonerate him from some of his crimes. He behaves like a dog because he lives in a 'dog eat dog' world.

CONSCIENCE

Linked to the theme of good and evil is the idea of conscience, which always has religious connotations in *Richard III*. The word appears frequently throughout the play. Until his dream on Bosworth field, Richard refuses to acknowledge that he has a conscience, just as he rejects religion. He believes that he is free of all moral constraints and can act as he pleases. This leads to his damnation. Gradually we come to realise the importance of conscience, which redeems those who repent. Richard is arguably destroyed by his own conscience when he wakes up from his nightmare the night before the final battle. Sweating and terrified, he is forced to confront the reality of something he chose to dismiss. This outcome was hinted at earlier by Anne when she informed us that her husband slept badly. Richmond, who sleeps soundly, has a clear conscience. Even if there does not seem to be much overt goodness to rely on in *Richard III*, the presentation of conscience suggests that God cannot be toyed with. Those who choose to ignore His laws will suffer terrible torment. There is a very clear moral lesson here: man must admit and act on his own powerful conscience.

PROVIDENCE & FREE WILL

Those who see *Richard III* as a play which accepts and presents a belief in Christian providence suggest that there can be no ambiguity about what occurs. Richard is destined to fail because he is damned. He is the final terrible link in the bloody chain of events that began with the Wars of the Roses. When he has inflicted God's punishment on England, he will be removed. The play undoubtedly insists on historical causation. In Act I Scene 3 Margaret and her enemies wrangle with each other about the crimes committed during the battles between the houses of Lancaster and York. The scenes involving the female characters are all used as opportunities to remind the audience of the brutal deaths that have afflicted the two principal families. Most significantly, there is the repeated use of prophecy to **foreshadow** Richard's fall. When he says that he is 'determined to prove a villain' (I.1.30), there is no doubt about the direction Richard is heading in. We know what the outcome of the play will be. We might be tempted to feel that Richard is little more than God's puppet.

However, Shakespeare also seems to suggest that man has some degree of choice. Buckingham and Hastings choose to ignore the warnings they · are offered, while Stanley chooses the path of righteousness when he defects to Richmond's cause. Richard has clearly made his choice before the play begins – he announces his evil intentions in Act I Scene 1. For three acts he is very much in control of events, making lightning and opportunistic decisions which bring him success. He looks – and sounds – invincible. In the second half of the play, as the wheel of fortune turns, Richard finds he has fewer choices. He has to react to the choices others make. Buckingham and Stanley desert him, and Elizabeth's daughter is not his for the asking. When his conscience pricks him, he fails to change direction. Unlike all his victims, he does not accept providence before he dies. He seems to want to insist that he can choose his own destiny right up to his final moment. We might feel that his destructive defiance is simultaneously foolhardy and courageous.

AMBITION, TYRANNY & THE NATURE OF KINGSHIP

A large number of Elizabethan and Jacobean plays explore the theme of kingship. **Tragedy** was traditionally a genre which dealt with the rise and fall of great men. Shakespeare's **histories** and tragedies all portray the machinations of princes and sovereigns. *Richard III* is interesting because it seems to embrace two opposing ideas about the right to rule. On the one hand there is the old medieval idea – the divine right of kings. A prince would inherit his father's crown because of his birthright, and, regardless of his behaviour and fitness to serve, the populace would be bound to obey him. Usurpation was a grave and sinful transgression of God's laws. However, other, less feudal views were emerging. It was increasingly felt by many that it was acceptable (but certainly not desirable) to rise against a king who showed himself to be tyrannical and

wicked. Although they were shocked by – and misinterpreted – some of
the ideas in *The Prince*, the Elizabethans were given a great deal of food
for thought when Niccolò **Machiavelli's** political work was published.
Here were some new and radical messages about gaining and maintaining
power. Put crudely, Machiavelli suggested that if you were manipulative
and clever, you deserved to have power, and that if you continued to act
in an intelligent manner, you could hang on to your authority. You
should use any means necessary to achieve your ends, and anything – even
murder – was acceptable, if it was efficacious.

So where does Richard III fit into this picture? Strangely, in spite
of the fact that he is a self-conscious usurper, driven by overweening
ambition, Richard seems to believe in the rights of succession. The
amoral, political schemer is also intensely feudal in outlook. Right from
the start he is interested in portraying himself as the rightful sovereign.
Richard slanders his dead brother Edward, Elizabeth, Clarence's children
– even his own mother – in order to present himself as his father's true
heir. Richard is concerned to maintain the appearance of legitimacy. He
knows that he must dispose of Edward's young sons if he is to remain on
the throne unchallenged. He must be the only male member of the house
of York left alive. Later he proposes to marry Elizabeth's daughter to
secure his throne, no doubt hoping to breed by her. This is at once a
political and dynastic marriage: Richard hopes that the Yorkist line will
prosper for many generations to come.

When he is challenged by Richmond, Richard responds with a
kind of medieval despotism. He has become increasingly tyrannical
throughout Act IV. It comes as no surprise to hear him dismiss
Richmond and his followers as 'vagabonds, rascals, and runaways …
overweening rags of France … bastard Bretons' (V.3.317–34) when he
makes his oration to his troops on Bosworth field. There is a fascinating
contradiction here. Richard originally set himself up as an antagonistic
'other', at odds with his family and the religious and political values of the
ruling elite. Now he speaks like a feudal reactionary, insisting on his own
and his followers' patriotism after a period of laying waste to the nobility
of England. Essentially Richard wants it both ways: he wants to be the
Machiavel, who achieves the crown through his own cunning and daring,
while simultaneously being treated as if he is God's anointed. But there
has always been a flaw in Richard's plans. He lusted after the crown for

its own sake; Shakespeare does not suggest that he had a clear idea of what he wanted to do once he achieved power. The villain's imagination fails him once he is king. His ambition becomes despotism and, like Macbeth, he finds that he is trapped in a cycle of slaughter with no way out. Richard suffers the same fate as countless ambitious and egotistical outsiders in Elizabethan and Jacobean dramas: he is destroyed by a more selfless and righteous revenger, a man who has God on his side. At the end of this play Shakespeare, like Richard, seems to want it both ways. Richmond, who is undoubtedly a usurper, is presented as the antidote to tyranny. The political manoeuvrings of the first three acts give way to a much more conservative portrait of a virtuous, old-fashioned ruler, who will take care of the nation in a paternalistic and selfless way. There are mixed messages about the nature of kingship in *Richard III*, not all of which can be reconciled with each other.

VENGEANCE & JUSTICE

This theme is closely linked to the previous one. Richmond can be viewed as a revenger, but he is God's revenger, sent to cleanse England and restore sanity. The dramatist makes it very plain that he is not operating out of personal ambition. Thus we can feel content that Richmond is an agent of divine justice. At the same time, we must recognise the justice of Richard's reign. Throughout the play Margaret recalls the crimes committed during the Wars of the Roses. Thus we are constantly reminded that Gloucester can be viewed as God's scourge. England must suffer for the cycle of destruction that the houses of Lancaster and York have inflicted on the nation since the usurpation of Richard II. All of the principal characters in the play are part of this evil history, and as a result we will feel, to some extent, that it is apt that they should suffer. This is **poetic justice**. Some critics would go so far as to say that they deserve the treatment Richard metes out to them. While this is debatable, it is surely not true that Edward's innocent sons deserve to be smothered in the Tower. It is this act of outrageous injustice that is the turning point in the play. This crime must be revenged. When he says that he will 'unite the white rose and the red' (V.5.19) by marrying the dead princes' sister, Richmond is promising a new line of kings, who will replace the unfortunate boys.

APPEARANCE & REALITY

This theme is dwelt on almost obsessively in the drama of the period.
Shakespeare returned to it many times, and not only in his **history plays**.
In *Richard III* we become aware of the deceptive nature of outward
appearances in the very first scene, when the villain announces his evil
intentions in an artful and self-conscious way. Immediately after his
opening **soliloquy** we watch Gloucester conceal his wickedness with a
convincing display of brotherly concern. Thereafter we are always aware
that we are watching an actor at work and we realise that we cannot trust
appearances. This is a lesson that many of the characters have to learn.
But in the meantime they – and we – are seduced by a consummate
performer.

Richard's false exterior helps him create the reality he desires. For
three acts it looks as if there is no role that Richard cannot play
successfully. All his moments of greatest triumph are intensely theatrical:
the wooing of Anne, the confrontation with Margaret, Hastings's
downfall, the scene where he reluctantly takes the crown. But after his
coronation, a theatrical ritual that has meaning regardless of Richard's
ability to play his part, the actor loses his place in the drama. He cannot
contain his evil and he goes too far. Those who allowed themselves to be
beguiled by his appearance begin to heed Margaret's warnings, and they
turn against the protagonist. It becomes apparent that Richard's
deformed body tells the truth. Is this is a comforting idea for the
audience? Having suggested that it is possible to deceive with flattering
words and looks, Shakespeare then seems to insist on the opposite. At the
end of the play we have to accept Richmond at face value and believe that
the virtues he professes to possess are real. This simplistic finale perhaps
sits uncomfortably with the sophisticated presentation of actors and
acting that has gone before.

IRONY

Richard III remains compelling today because of the dramatist's extensive
and sophisticated use of **irony**. This play is full of verbal and situational
irony. Of all Shakespeare's protagonists, Richard is perhaps the most

knowing. His witty **asides** and soliloquies draw us in. For three acts the villain's tongue is firmly in his cheek as he comments on his own and others' beliefs and actions. Richard knows more than anyone else onstage for most of the play, and he makes devastating use of his knowledge. But ultimately the joke is on him. The ironist cannot see the **dramatic irony** of his own situation – he is destined to fail because he is evil. In the second half of the play irony works against Richard. The women he despises rail and, in Elizabeth's case, conspire against him. His trusted henchman Buckingham, without whom he could not have achieved the crown, deserts him. Stanley proves to possess Ricardian cunning and, ultimately, the usurper is usurped by a scion of the house of Lancaster he thought he had destroyed when he murdered Henry VI. The atheist who thought he was in control of time and his own destiny is destroyed by God's champion. Thus irony is closely linked to the theme of justice in *Richard III*.

PART FOUR

TEXTUAL ANALYSIS

TEXT 1 HASTINGS'S DOWNFALL (III.4.21–79)

Enter RICHARD.

ELY: In happy time, here comes the Duke himself.

RICHARD: My noble lords and cousins all, good morrow:
I have been long a sleeper, but I trust
My absence doth neglect no great design
Which by my presence might have been concluded.   25

BUCKINGHAM: Had you not come upon your cue, my lord,
William Lord Hastings had pronounc'd your part –
I mean your voice for crowning of the King.

RICHARD: Than my Lord Hastings no man might be bolder:
His lordship knows me well, and loves me well.   30
My Lord of Ely, when I was last in Holborn
I saw good strawberries in your garden there;
I do beseech you, send for some of them.

ELY: Marry, and will, my lord, with all my heart.   *Exit.*

RICHARD: Cousin of Buckingham, a word with you.   35
Catesby hath sounded Hastings in our business,
And finds the testy gentleman so hot
That he will lose his head ere give consent
His master's child (as worshipfully he terms it)
Shall lose the royalty of England's throne.   40

BUCKINGHAM: Withdraw yourself a while: I'll go with you.
                         Exeunt [RICHARD *and* BUCKINGHAM].

STANLEY: We have not yet set down this day of triumph.
Tomorrow, in my judgement, is too sudden,
For I myself am not so well provided
As else I would be, were the day prolong'd.   45

Enter BISHOP OF ELY.

ELY: Where is my lord the Duke of Gloucester?
I have sent for these strawberries.

HASTINGS: His Grace looks cheerfully and smooth today:
There's some conceit or other likes him well
When that he bids good morrow with such spirit.   50
I think there's never a man in Christendom
Can lesser hide his love or hate than he,
For by his face straight shall you know his heart.

STANLEY: What of his heart perceive you in his face
By any livelihood he show'd today?   55

HASTINGS: Marry, that with no man here he is offended,
For were he, he had shown it in his looks.

STANLEY: I pray God he be not, I say.

Enter RICHARD *and* BUCKINGHAM.

RICHARD: I pray you all, tell me what they deserve
That do conspire my death with devilish plots   60
Of damned witchcraft, and that have prevail'd
Upon my body with their hellish charms?

HASTINGS: The tender love I bear your Grace, my lord,
Makes me most forward in this princely presence,
To doom th'offenders, whatso'er they be: 65
I say, my lord, they have deserved death.

RICHARD: Then be your eyes the witness of their evil.
See how I am bewitch'd! Behold, mine arm
Is like a blasted sapling wither'd up!
And this is Edward's wife, that monstrous witch,   70
Consorted with that harlot, strumpet Shore,
That by their witchcraft thus have marked me.

HASTINGS: If they have done this deed, my noble lord –

RICHARD: If? Thou protector of this damned strumpet,
Talk'st thou to me of ifs! Thou art a traitor: 75

> Off with his head! Now by Saint Paul I swear
> I will not dine until I see the same.
> Lovell and Ratcliffe, look that it be done;
> The rest that love me, rise and follow me.

Act III Scene 4 opens on an **ironic** note. Hastings believes that he knows Richard's mind. As we suspect, he could not be more wrong. In this extract we watch as the foolish councillor is confronted by the truth and condemned to death.

Gloucester's entrance is as laden with irony as almost every other utterance and action in this scene. The Bishop of Ely announces that he arrives 'In happy time' (line 21). By the end of the scene Ely and his fellow councillors will troop out after the Protector in fear of their lives, and far from content. Ely's is unconscious irony, like Hastings's; but, as we shall see, there is a good deal of conscious irony in this scene too. Appropriately it is the manipulator Richard who makes good use of it. He begins with his customary feigned bonhomie, and the usual disclaimer of his own worth. This hypocritical talk will reach its apogee when he accepts the throne at the end of Act III, all the while protesting that he is 'unfit for state and majesty' (III.7.204). Is Richard getting in some useful public-speaking practice here? It is extremely ironic that he should claim that his absence has not been important; as we know, the personal 'great design' (line 24) the villain has in mind (usurpation) can only be 'concluded' by his 'presence' (line 25), because success depends upon his ability to act his part convincingly. As usual, Richard's agenda is both hidden and at odds with the desires and expectations of those around him.

Richard's power is increased because he has an ally. Buckingham's utterances add to the self-conscious and very theatrical irony of the scene. He declares that it is a good thing that Richard has 'come upon your cue' (line 26), reminding the audience that this event, like so many in this play, is stage-managed by the protagonist, who has found an able supporting actor to assist him. As we watch Richard and his henchman in action in this scene we are being prepared for their masterly double act in Act III Scene 7. The irony continues as Richard calls Hastings bold (line 29). Indeed he is. But – as is appropriate in a world that is being turned upside down by an evil demon – his bravery is fatal and unwitting: he has refused to support Gloucester's claim to the throne.

The tension increases steadily. Does Shakespeare add to or deflect it when he has Richard digress at line 31? The request for strawberries is typical of Richard's tactics; he knows when to change the topic in order to throw his listeners off balance. By this point in the play we know that he is most dangerous when he appears to be speaking casually. Here the innocuous question seems to confirm that Richard is in a light-hearted mood; thus his lightning change at line 59 will come as a great surprise, catching the councillors unawares. Ely's eager delight to comply and the confidence that he and Hastings profess to have in Richard demonstrate how successful the villain has been in fooling the peers of the realm. We also recognise that these simpletons will be wholly unprepared – and unfit – to deal with evil when it is revealed to them. The council members are no match for Gloucester.

Richard's contempt for his next victim is conveyed in his speech at line 35, especially in these two phrases: 'the testy gentleman' and 'His master's child (as worshipfully he terms it)' (lines 37–9). He seems to be parodying the pompous speech of the nobles, reminding us that he is both an effective rhetorician and the master of many styles of speech. Richard will need all the verbal skill he can muster in Act III Scene 7, when his audience will be a good deal less accommodating than the peers he toys with at the Tower.

But there is one dissenter. Stanley attempts to voice his concerns, wisely stopping short of making concrete objections to the plans that are being drawn up. His uncertainty shows that he has not been taken in. We are already inclined to trust Stanley's judgement. His ominous nightmare about the boar, alluded to in Act III Scene 2 – and again at the end of this scene – is, like all the other dreams and prophecies in *Richard III*, disturbingly apt and accurate. As the play proceeds Stanley's disapproval will become active resistance; thus his stature will increase. Ultimately he will play a major role in defeating the usurper. In a scene which becomes more alarming by the moment, it must be a relief for the audience to see that there is one nobleman who seems to possess moral integrity. Stanley represents hope: his lone voice suggests that evil will not prevail. His disquiet also prevents us from being seduced by Richard's powerful presence. It is easy to be carried away by the wicked, witty protagonist, even when he behaves like a tyrant, as he does in this extract. If we accept that one of the purposes of this **history play** is to serve as a moral lesson, then we must not side with Gloucester. We can find him amusing, we can even share in his contempt for some of his gullible victims, but we must not condone Richard's outrageous actions. Stanley reminds us of this. He speaks ironically to Hastings at line 54, intending to alert him to the danger of trusting in appearances, and then, in response to Hastings's comment that Richard is offended 'with no man here' (line 56), mutters ominously: 'I pray God he be not' (line 58).

But it is too late. Hastings lacks Stanley's cautious detachment and remains cheerful and complacent. Because the extract is loaded with irony and we have superior knowledge, it is easy to smile at Hastings's foolishness. We know that this kind of **hubris** comes before a fall. But surely Hastings does not deserve the fate that awaits him? Shakespeare makes this clear when Richard re-enters. The charge of treason is shocking because it is ludicrous, and completely unsubstantiated. It is a measure of Richard's skill as an actor that he prevails here. Of course, the weak dupes that make up the council help him, as do Lovell and Ratcliffe. Arguably, without the silence of one party, and the assistance of his henchmen, Richard could not dispose of Hastings. Nevertheless, Shakespeare puts Richard centre stage for a brief but bravura performance. At line 59 he makes use of one of his favourite techniques – the loaded question. Thus he sets up and ensnares his victim. Like Anne before him, Hastings takes Richard's words at face value and participates in his own ruin. It is sadly ironic that it is an empty question that seals Hastings's fate; here he gives what he believes will be the desired response, but it is hopeless because he gave the wrong answer when he was questioned by Catesby in Act III Scene 2. Even more ironically, Buckingham, who is a willing accomplice here, will also be undone when he fails to respond favourably to Richard's most vile request in Act IV Scene 2.

The rest of Richard's violent outburst is brilliantly controlled and intense, full of hysterical exaggeration and snap judgements. Its brevity makes it irresistible. Gloucester does not give the company time to think, and he rides over Hastings's protestations without any difficulty. In fact, he uses his words against him (another technique that makes him so effective). It is ironic that Richard should declare that 'devilish' witchcraft has been used against him: he is the real devil here. Having seen how masterfully he manipulated Anne in Act I, we will not be surprised to see him again abusing women to further his ambitions.

But we need to consider Richard's claim – that his arm has withered up as a result of Mistress Shore's spells – more closely. It is clearly preposterous. The Elizabethan audience, familiar with the Tudor myth of the demon Richard III, deformed hunchback, knew this was nonsense. The members of the council, like all the other characters in the play, know it is nonsense. Richard drew attention to his deformity in the opening **soliloquy**: he has not suddenly been blighted. So what point is Shakespeare making? Is he trying to suggest that Richard is so devilishly powerful he can make others accept whatever version of reality he chooses to assert? Or is he undermining the council members, showing us how fallible they are? Does their silence in the face of this outrageous false claim make them accessories to murder? Elsewhere in his dramatic oeuvre Shakespeare explores the idea that wicked men triumph when weak men remain silent. Whatever conclusion we reach in this scene, we are being prepared for Richard's greatest performance in Act III Scene 7 when he appears before the Lord Mayor and the citizens of London.

We cannot be surprised by the council's stunned silence, however. Richard reveals his murderous nature in a sudden and autocratic command: 'Off with his head!' (line 76), and leaves with another: 'The rest that love me, rise and follow me' (line 79). These words also function as a thinly veiled threat. The choice is clear: you are either Richard's friend or his enemy. Given the rapidity of Hastings's fall, only a madman would oppose the Protector at this moment. Richard's last line reveals the villain's egotism ('me' is repeated and stressed) and his resolution. It is a forceful, balanced line. The brutal speed of his actions and the intensity of the lines he speaks after his second entrance enable Richard to force the pace throughout the second part of this extract. At the moment time is on his side; he thinks fast, moves quickly and gets results partly because he is more alert than any of the other characters. The reference to dinner that Richard makes at line 77 sums up his restless ambition. Ironically he will have no appetite at all the night before

Text 1 continued

the Battle of Bosworth. And of course, his fall will be almost as swift as Hastings's.

TEXT 2   MARGARET'S FINAL APPEARANCE (IV.4.79–135)

ELIZABETH: O, thou didst prophesy the time would come
That I should wish for thee to help me curse   80
That bottled spider, that foul bunch-back'd toad.

MARGARET: I call'd thee then vain flourish of my fortune;
I call'd thee, then, poor shadow, painted queen,
The presentation of but what I was;
The flattering index of a direful pageant;   85
One heav'd a-high, to be hurl'd down below;
A mother only mock'd with two fair babes;
A dream of what thou wast; a garish flag
To be the aim of every dangerous shot;
A sign of dignity; a breath, a bubble;   90
A queen in jest, only to fill the scene.
Where is thy husband now? Where be thy brothers?
Where are thy two sons? Wherein dost thou joy?
Who sues, and kneels, and says 'God save the Queen'?
Where be the bending peers that flatter'd thee?   95
Where be the thronging troops that follow'd thee?
Decline all this, and see what now thou art:
For happy wife, a most distressed widow;
For joyful mother, one that wails the name;
For one being sued to, one that humbly sues;   100
For Queen, a very caitiff, crown'd with care;
For she that scorn'd at me, now scorn'd of me;
For she being fear'd of all, now fearing one;
For she commanding all, obey'd of none.
Thus hath the course of justice whirl'd about   105
And left thee but a very prey to time,
Having no more but thought of what thou wast
To torture thee the more, being what thou art.

Thou didst usurp my place, and dost thou not
Usurp the just proportion of my sorrow?   110
Now thy proud neck bears half my burden'd yoke,
From which even here I slip my weary head,
And leave the burden of it all on thee.
Farewell, York's wife, and Queen of sad mischance;
These English woes shall make me smile in France.   115

ELIZABETH: O thou, well skill'd in curses, stay awhile
And teach me how to curse mine enemies.

MARGARET: Forbear to sleep the nights, and fast the days;
Compare dead happiness with living woe;
Think that thy babes were sweeter than they were,   120
And he that slew them fouler than he is:
Bettering thy loss makes the bad-causer worse.
Revolving this will teach thee how to curse.

ELIZABETH: My words are dull: O quicken them with thine.

MARGARET: Thy woes will make them sharp and pierce like mine.   125
                                                         Exit.

DUCHESS: Why should calamity be full of words?

ELIZABETH: Windy attorneys to their clients' woes,
Airy succeeders of intestate joys,
Poor breathing orators of miseries:
Let them have scope, though what they will impart   130
Help nothing else, yet do they ease the heart.

DUCHESS: If so, then be not tongue-tied; go with me
And in the breath of bitter words let's smother
My damned son, that thy two sweet sons smother'd.
The trumpet sounds; be copious in exclaims.   135

Here we see three royal ladies in lamentation. It is a scene we have
become familiar with. Throughout *Richard III* the female characters have
been used as a **chorus** to comment on Richard's character and the dire –
personal and political – consequences of his rise to power. This extract is
no different, although there is a new, fragile note of harmony. Previously

the women – especially Margaret and Elizabeth – have been at odds. This has not been surprising, since their allegiances are different. It is also a characteristic of lamentation scenes that the characters should compete with each other as they express the intensity of their grief. Here, although Margaret is still, to some extent, carping from the sidelines, she also seems to move closer to the other women. We readily recognise that all three characters onstage share the same predicament. They have been 'hurl'd down below' (line 86) by the events that have occurred; they have all had to deal with the deaths of their 'fair babes' (line 87) and husbands; they are all now 'distressed' (line 98) widows, who have been mocked and tormented by Richard of Gloucester.

Elizabeth's despairing acknowledgement of Margaret's prophecies immediately suggests that she has come to accept the embittered former queen's viewpoint. As the extract continues she will even seek her help: 'teach me how to curse mine enemies' (line 117). She recognises Margaret's power. We are also reminded that the only power the women in this play have is to curse. So far they have been victims; thus it is appropriate that the majority of scenes in which we see them show them frozen and static, raging against what has happened but unable to do anything to influence the course of events. Nonetheless, their words have a significant impact on the audience. We are offered full and vivid descriptions of the women's woes, and the repetitive quality of these lamentation scenes, in which the same points and emotions are explored, has a cumulative effect. Shakespeare wishes us to see how wretched England is under Richard's rule, and these despairing women help him to keep this idea in our minds. The lamentation scenes also contrast vividly with the more energetic and swift-moving scenes when Richard is onstage; thus the playwright adds to the dramatic interest of the play by changing the tone and pace.

What are we to make of Margaret's final speech? She remains personally antipathetic towards Elizabeth, calling her 'poor shadow, painted queen' (line 83) and 'A queen in jest' (line 91). Her mocking rhetorical questions (lines 92–6) are characteristically vindictive, but throughout this speech Margaret is also making more general points. She reminds us of the long 'course of justice' (line 105) that will bring Richard III's bloody career to an end. Her talk of usurpation reminds us of the exhaustive cycle of the Wars of the Roses, which will shortly come to a climax on Bosworth field. It is fitting that she should leave as she entered, offering bitter and cruel advice. But she is not an unwelcome guest now. The other women listen to her – perhaps eagerly. They appreciate how 'well skill'd in curses' (line 116) she is. The finality of her last rhyming couplet – two lines which end with negative words – is entirely appropriate to the speaker and to England's state: 'worse' and 'curse' (lines 122–3) sum Margaret up. Thus her role as prophetess comes to a close. But there is another woman ready to step into her shoes when Margaret retires to France. This point is driven home when Margaret's last line in the play rhymes with one of Elizabeth's: 'mine' rhymes with 'thine' (lines 124–5). These words suggest that Elizabeth is ready to assume Margaret's role. Are the two former queens in harmony at this point? Elizabeth says she wants to curse, and Margaret acknowledges that her woes will enable her to do this. It could be argued that there is finally an equality of grief, a recognition of each other's misery.

The woe continues after Margaret departs. The Duchess of York seems to have lost heart. At line 126 she questions the efficacy of wailing and cursing. Elizabeth replies that words can 'ease the heart' (line 131), reminding us of the purpose of these lamentation scenes. They are cathartic: for speaker, listener and audience. The duchess rallies and speaks with more resolution (conveyed by the alliteration of t, b and s in the speech at line 132). Her desire to describe her 'calamity' (an extremely powerful word) prepares us for the confrontation she and Elizabeth will shortly have with Richard. And this time, because the women are focused and share the same intentions, we know the wily protagonist will not triumph over them as easily as he wooed the lone Anne in Act I.

Misery has made these women strong. We know that Elizabeth, like Margaret, is a survivor. In the scenes that follow we will come to realise that she is no lily-livered bystander and that she has learnt from her mistakes. Here she buoys up and joins with her mother-in-law, preparing to take on their common enemy. Soon she will contrive a way to protect her daughter, having been unable to save her young sons. When she promises young Elizabeth of York to Richmond she will play an active part in history, helping to establish the Tudor dynasty. Even the Duchess of York, who seems to be a broken old woman in many ways, will find the strength to reject and denounce her abominable son in the

TEXT 2 continued

public street. It is fitting that this extract should end on an urgent and energetic note, as the women prepare for verbal battle. Their encounter with the venomous Margaret has whetted their appetite for more cursing.

TEXT 3 RICHARD'S DREAM (V.3.178–237)

RICHARD *starteth up out of a dream.*

KING RICHARD: Give me another horse! Bind up my wounds!
Have mercy, Jesu! – Soft, I did but dream.
O coward conscience, how dost thou afflict me!   180
The lights burn blue; it is now dead midnight.
Cold fearful drops stand on my trembling flesh.
What do I fear? Myself? There's none else by;
Richard loves Richard, that is, I and I.
Is there a murderer here? No. Yes, I am!   185
Then fly. What, from myself? Great reason why,
Lest I revenge? What, myself upon myself?
Alack, I love myself. Wherefore? For any good
That I myself have done unto myself?
O no, alas, I rather hate myself   190
For hateful deeds committed by myself.
I am a villain – yet I lie, I am not!
Fool, of thyself speak well! Fool, do not flatter.
My conscience hath a thousand several tongues,
And every tongue brings in a several tale,   195
And every tale condemns me for a villain:
Perjury, perjury, in the highest degree;
Murder, stern murder, in the direst degree;
All several sins, all us'd in each degree,
Throng to the bar, crying all, 'Guilty, guilty!'   200
I shall despair. There is no creature loves me,
And if I die, no soul will pity me –
And wherefore should they, since that I myself
Find in myself no pity to myself?
Methought the souls of all that I had murder'd   205

Came to my tent, and every one did threat
Tomorrow's vengeance on the head of Richard.

Enter RATCLIFFE.

RATCLIFFE: My lord!

KING RICHARD: Zounds! Who is there?

RATCLIFFE: Ratcliffe, my lord; 'tis I. The early village cock   210
Hath twice done salutation to the morn;
Your friends are up and buckle on their armour.

KING RICHARD: O Ratcliffe, I have dream'd a fearful dream!
What thinkest thou – will our friends prove all true?

RATCLIFFE: No doubt, my lord.

KING RICHARD: O Ratcliffe, I fear, I fear!   215

RATCLIFFE: Nay, good my lord, be not afraid of shadows.

KING RICHARD: By the Apostle Paul, shadows tonight
Have struck more terror to the soul of Richard
Than can the substance of ten thousand soldiers,
Armed in proof, and led by shallow Richmond.   220
'Tis not yet near day; come, go with me:
Under our tents I'll play the eavesdropper,
To see if any mean to shrink from me.
                    Exeunt RICHARD *and* RATCLIFFE.

Enter the LORDS *to* RICHMOND *sitting in his tent.*

LORDS: Good morrow, Richmond.

RICHMOND: Cry mercy, lords and watchful gentlemen,   225
That you have ta'en a tardy sluggard here.

I LORD: How have you slept, my lord?

RICHMOND: The sweetest sleep and fairest-boding dreams
That ever enter'd in a drowsy head
Have I, since your departure, had, my lords.   230
Methought their souls whose bodies Richard murder'd

Came to my tent and cried on victory.
I promise you my soul is very jocund
In the remembrance of so fair a dream.
How far into the morning is it, lords?   235

I LORD: Upon the stroke of four.

RICHMOND: Why then 'tis time to arm and give direction

Richard seems to wake at a moment close to death. His last words in the
play will be 'A horse! A horse! My kingdom for a horse!' (V.4.13), so his
first line in this extract clearly **foreshadows** his end. Our sense that
Richard is on his deathbed is increased by his plea for mercy, and because
we have just heard him condemned by the ghosts of his victims.
However, is Richard speaking consciously here? Shakespeare's lines
suggest that he is only fully awake when he says, 'Soft, I did but dream'
(line 179). This is his first attempt at calming himself. But surely his
mind is shattered? The physical details the protagonist describes create
this impression – the blue light, the dark night and the sweat on his
'trembling flesh' (line 182) all point to an atmosphere of cold terror. The
fractured syntax of the lines and the series of questions and answers
confirm his mental agitation.

Richard seems to be arguing with himself at lines 183–93. He
sees himself clearly for what he is: a loveless murderer. But at the same
time he seems to be trying to defend himself against an accuser. Is
Shakespeare trying to suggest a divided self? That the previously
resolute and brutal villain has a God-fearing heart? That, to use a
psychologist's term, Richard has been 'in denial' for four acts? Perhaps
not. When he is fully conscious he does not appeal to God to save him,
a point that will be discussed below. What Richard's words certainly
suggest is that he is coming closer to sharing the negative view of
himself held by his victims and enemies: 'Alack, I love myself … O no,
alas, I rather hate myself / For hateful deeds committed by myself'
(lines 188–91). There is distance and dislocation in these words. We
understand that the villain's conscience – something we did not suspect
he possessed – has finally assaulted him. The vivid **personification** of his
conscience at line 194 confirms its power and again points to dislocation,
as does the feverish, repetitive phrasing of lines 195–200. This

introspection is striking because it is so novel. The villain has never consulted his feelings or questioned his actions before. He has simply been intent on evil. The closest he came to introspection was in Act IV Scene 2, when he mused about his destiny. But now he is fearful, of himself, and what he has done. He echoes the words of the ghosts when he declares, 'I shall despair' (line 201). The schizophrenia of so many of the utterances we hear suggests that the protagonist is fatally weakened, even before he has gone into battle.

The speech ends with a brief recollection of the details of the dream. Thus all the prophecies made by Margaret and Richard's other victims are justified. The audience must feel some satisfaction in seeing the villain forced to face up to his sins. It is particularly apt that this happens when he is alone. From the outset of the play he has set himself up as an isolated and egotistical 'other', whose values and ambitions are at odds with everyone else's. Appropriately he will die alone, on foot, in the midst of the battle. His isolation is now an affliction, and a sign of Richard's weakness, rather than a strength.

However, in spite of the evidence we have that Richard is no longer impregnable, he nevertheless retains some of his villainous strength of mind. His speech becomes more sombre and perhaps there are even hints of self-pity when he says 'no creature loves me' (line 201), but, significantly, Richard does not beg God to pardon him when he speaks of his 'several sins' (line 199) and considers the battle to come. We are being prepared for the moment when he will say that he is ready to go 'to hell' at line 314. Even now, when he is afraid, the villain remains on the course he set himself when he began plotting at the start of the play. Unlike his victims, Richard does not repent when he has the chance. He recognises his evil, acknowledges the power of his conscience, but he is not really a changed man at the end of this speech. Because of this, we find it hard to sympathise with the devil. Increasingly we feel distanced from Richard III, because we recognise that the world will not be losing anything good or worthy when he dies. Quite the contrary. As this speech makes clear, England will be a safer place without this murderer. It is necessary for us to believe that Richard's death is appropriate if we are to see Richmond's triumph as a positive event. His failure to make peace with God shows us that the villain must be physically defeated, as he has now been defeated, mentally, by a dream.

Shakespeare makes very effective use of Ratcliffe's entrance to change the brooding tone and increase the tension. Like Richard, we jump when Ratcliffe cries, 'My lord!' (line 208). Shaken, the villain utters a characteristic oath and seems on the point of confiding in his companion, but he stops short at the end of line 213, changing the topic. But we know he is not fully in control of himself, as he was throughout every exchange he participated in during the first three acts of the play, when he changed topics in order to assert his will and further his aims. Now he asks a question which reveals his uncertainty: 'will our friends prove all true?' (line 214). In the past Richard did not need reassurance from his inferiors. We recognise the **irony** of the question; Richard has just been speaking about his friendless isolation, and now he desperately seems to need friends. In spite of Ratcliffe's rather feeble assurances, Richard remains disconcerted. He cannot forget his dream at lines 215–20. This is satisfying. We know he is right to be 'afraid of shadows' because the ghosts' prophecies will be as accurate as all the other prophecies in this play. Again there is an irony here; but now the irony is working against Richard. He was the shadow at the start of the play; now the shadowy ghosts have made him more fearful than he would ever have believed possible. But thoughts of 'shallow' Richmond finally enable him to rouse himself, and some of Richard's old bravery and insouciance return. His contempt for his enemy is clear at line 220. He seems mentally prepared to do battle with thousands of soldiers. In daylight he will not be cowardly. But it remains ironic that he should have been so shaken by the dead souls of those he despised in life; the living enemy he dismisses as 'shallow' will prove to be his nemesis.

Richard's final lines in this extract suggest that the arch manipulator has now sunk to pettiness. He intends to eavesdrop on his soldiers to find out if they are still loyal to him. Does this show that Richard is pessimistic about the outcome of the battle? By way of contrast, Richmond is optimistic. He has slept soundly, and is well pleased with the 'fairest-boding dreams' (line 228) he has had. His undisturbed rest suggests that his conscience, unlike Richard's, is clear. Richmond also speaks of his 'jocund' (line 233) soul. Even at his lowest point in his **soliloquy**, Richard was unable speak of his own soul, suggesting that he does not have one; he merely spoke of the souls of the dead and the living souls who will not be able to pity him when he dies. Finally, Richmond's last line in this extract is very different from Richard's. He speaks confidently of giving his army 'direction' (line 237); he does not need to spy on his men because he has every confidence in them, in his righteous cause and in his destiny. By the end of this extract we know that Richard is doomed. And he has, in many ways, shown that he recognises this.

PART FIVE

BACKGROUND

WILLIAM SHAKESPEARE'S LIFE

There are no personal records of Shakespeare's life. Official documents and occasional references to him by contemporary dramatists enable us to draw the main outline of his public life, but his private life remains hidden. Although not at all unusual for a writer of his time, this lack of first-hand evidence has tempted many to read his plays as personal records and to look in them for clues to his character and convictions. The results are unconvincing, partly because Renaissance art was not subjective or designed primarily to express its creator's personality, and partly because the drama of any period is very difficult to read biographically. Except when plays are written by committed dramatists to promote social or political causes (as by Shaw or Brecht), it is all but impossible to decide who amongst the variety of fictional characters in a drama represents the dramatist, or which of the various and often conflicting points of view expressed is authorial.

What we do know can be quickly summarised. Shakespeare was born into a well-to-do family in the market town of Stratford-upon-Avon in Warwickshire, where he was baptised, in Holy Trinity Church, on 26 April 1564. His father, John Shakespeare, was a prosperous glover and leather merchant who became a person of some importance in the town: in 1565 he was elected an alderman of the town, and in 1568 he became high bailiff (or mayor) of Stratford. In 1557 he had married Mary Arden. Their third child (of eight) and eldest son, William, learnt to read and write at the primary (or 'petty') school in Stratford and then, it seems probable, attended the local grammar school, where he would have studied Latin, history, logic and rhetoric. In November 1582 William, then aged eighteen, married Anne Hathaway, who was twenty-six years old. They had a daughter, Susanna, in May 1583, and twins, Hamnet and Judith, in 1585.

Shakespeare next appears in the historical record in 1592 when he was mentioned as a London actor and playwright in a pamphlet by the dramatist Robert Greene. These 'lost years' 1585–92 have been the subject of much speculation, but how they were occupied remains as much a mystery as when Shakespeare left Stratford, and why. In his pamphlet, *Greene's Groatsworth of Wit*, Greene expresses to his fellow dramatists his outrage that the 'upstart crow' Shakespeare has the impudence to believe he 'is as well able to bombast out a **blank verse** as the best of you'. To have aroused this hostility from a rival, Shakespeare must, by 1592, have been long enough in London to have made a name for himself as a playwright. We may conjecture that he had left Stratford in 1586 or 1587.

During the next twenty years, Shakespeare continued to live in London, regularly visiting his wife and family in Stratford. He continued to act, but his chief fame was as a dramatist. From 1594 he wrote exclusively for the Lord Chamberlain's Men, which rapidly became the leading dramatic company and from 1603 enjoyed the patronage of James I as the King's Men. His plays were extremely popular and he became a shareholder in his theatre company. He was able to buy lands around Stratford and a large house in the town, to which he retired about 1611. He died there on 23 April 1616 and was buried in Holy Trinity Church on 25 April.

SHAKESPEARE'S DRAMATIC CAREER

Between the late 1580s and 1613 Shakespeare wrote thirty-seven plays, and contributed to some by other dramatists. This was by no means an exceptional number for a professional playwright of the times. The exact date of the composition of individual plays is a matter of debate – for only a few plays is the date of their first performance known – but the broad outlines of Shakespeare's dramatic career have been established. He began in the late 1580s and early 1590s by rewriting earlier plays and working with plotlines inspired by the Classics. He concentrated on comedies (such as *The Comedy of Errors*, 1590–4, which derived from the Latin playwright Plautus) and plays dealing with English history (such as the three parts of *Henry VI*, 1589–92), though he also tried his hand at bloodthirsty **revenge tragedy** (*Titus Andronicus*, 1592–3, indebted to both Ovid and Seneca). During the 1590s Shakespeare developed his expertise in these kinds of play to write comic masterpieces such as *A Midsummer*

Night's Dream (1594–5) and *As You Like It* (1599–1600) and **history plays** such as *Henry IV* (1596–8) and *Henry V* (1598–9).

As the new century begins a new note is detectable. Plays such as *Troilus and Cressida* (1601–2) and *Measure for Measure* (1603–4), poised between comedy and **tragedy**, evoke complex responses. Because of their generic uncertainty and ambivalent tone such works are sometimes referred to as 'problem plays', but it is tragedy which comes to dominate the extraordinary sequence of masterpieces: *Hamlet* (1600–1), *Othello* (1602–4), *King Lear* (1605–6), *Macbeth* (1605–6) and *Antony and Cleopatra* (1606).

In the last years of his dramatic career, Shakespeare wrote a group of plays of a quite different kind. These 'romances', as they are often called, are in many ways the most remarkable of all his plays. The group comprises *Pericles* (1608), *Cymbeline* (1609–11), *The Winter's Tale* (1610–11) and *The Tempest* (1610–11). These plays (particularly *Cymbeline*) reprise many of the situations and themes of the earlier dramas but in fantastical and exotic dramatic designs which, set in distant lands, covering large tracts of time and involving music, mime, dance and tableaux, have something of the qualities of masques and pageants. The situations which in the tragedies had led to disaster are here resolved: the great theme is restoration and reconciliation. Where in the tragedies Ophelia, Desdemona and Cordelia died, the daughters of these plays – Marina, Imogen, Perdita, Miranda – survive and are reunited with their parents and lovers.

THE TEXTS OF SHAKESPEARE'S PLAYS

Nineteen of Shakespeare's plays were printed during his lifetime in what are called 'quartos' (books, each containing one play, and made up of sheets of paper each folded twice to make four leaves). Shakespeare, however, did not supervise their publication. This was not unusual. When a playwright had sold a play to a dramatic company he sold his rights in it: copyright belonged to whoever had possession of an actual copy of the text, and so consequently authors had no control over what happened to their work. Anyone who could get hold of the text of a play might publish it if they wished. Hence, what found its way into print might be the author's copy, but it might be an actor's copy or prompt copy, perhaps cut or altered for performance; sometimes, actors (or even members of the audience) might publish what they could remember of the text. Printers, working without the benefit of the author's oversight, introduced their own errors, through misreading the manuscript, for example, and by 'correcting' what seemed to them not to make sense.

In 1623 John Heminges and Henry Condell, two actors in Shakespeare's company, collected together texts of thirty-six of Shakespeare's plays (*Pericles* was omitted) and published them in a large folio (a book in which each sheet of paper is folded once in half, to give two leaves). This, the First Folio, was followed by later editions in 1632, 1663 and 1685. Despite its appearance of authority, however, the texts in the First Folio still present many difficulties, for there are printing errors and confused passages in the plays, and its texts often differ significantly from those of the earlier quartos, when these exist.

Shakespeare's texts have, then, been through a number of intermediaries. We do not have his authority for any one of his plays, and hence we cannot know exactly what it was that he wrote. Bibliographers, textual critics and editors have spent a great deal of effort on endeavouring to get behind the errors, uncertainties and contradictions in the available texts to recover the plays as Shakespeare originally wrote them. What we read is the result of these efforts. Modern texts are what editors have constructed from the available evidence: they correspond to no sixteenth- or seventeenth-century editions, and to no early performance of a Shakespeare play. Furthermore, these composite texts differ from each other, for different editors read the early texts differently and come to different conclusions. A Shakespeare text is an unstable and a contrived thing.

Often, of course, its judgements embody, if not the personal prejudices of the editor, then the cultural preferences of the time in which he or she was working. Growing awareness of this has led recent scholars to distrust the whole editorial enterprise and to repudiate the attempt to construct a 'perfect' text. Stanley Wells and Gary Taylor, the editors of the Oxford edition of *The Complete Works* (1988), point out that almost certainly the texts of Shakespeare's plays were altered in performance, and from one performance to another, so that there may never have been a single version. They note, too, that Shakespeare probably revised and rewrote some plays. They do not claim to print a definitive text of any play, but prefer what seems to them the 'more theatrical' version, and when there is a great difference between available versions, as with *King Lear*, they print two texts.

SHAKESPEARE & THE ENGLISH RENAISSANCE

Shakespeare arrived in London at the very time that the Elizabethan period was poised to become the 'golden age' of English literature. Although Elizabeth reigned as queen from 1558 to 1603, the term 'Elizabethan' is used very loosely in a literary sense to refer to the period 1580 to 1625, when the great works of the age were produced. (Sometimes the later part of this period is distinguished as 'Jacobean', from the Latin form of the name of the king who succeeded Elizabeth, James I of England and VI of Scotland, who reigned from 1603 to 1625.) The poet Edmund Spenser heralded this new age with his pastoral poem *The Shepheardes Calender* (1579) and in his essay *An Apologie for Poetrie* (written about 1580, although not published until 1595) his friend Sir Philip Sidney championed the imaginative power of the 'speaking picture of poesy', famously declaring that 'Nature never set forth the earth in so rich a tapestry as divers poets have done ... Her world is brazen, the poet's only deliver a golden'.

Spenser and Sidney were part of that rejuvenating movement in European culture which since the nineteenth century has been known by the term 'Renaissance'. Meaning literally 'rebirth' it denotes a revival and redirection of artistic and intellectual endeavour which began in Italy in the fourteenth century in the poetry of Petrarch. It spread gradually northwards across Europe, and is first detectable in England in the early sixteenth century in the writings of the scholar and statesman Sir Thomas More and in the poetry of Sir Thomas Wyatt and Henry Howard, Earl of Surrey. Its keynote was a curiosity in thought which challenged old assumptions and traditions. To the innovative spirit of the Renaissance, the preceding ages appeared dully unoriginal and conformist.

That spirit was fuelled by the rediscovery of many Classical texts and the culture of Greece and Rome. This fostered a confidence in human reason and in human potential which, in every sphere, challenged old convictions. The discovery of America and its peoples (Columbus had sailed in 1492) demonstrated that the world was a larger and stranger place than had been thought. The cosmological speculation of Copernicus (later confirmed by Galileo) that the sun, not the earth, was the centre of our planetary system challenged the centuries-old belief that the earth and human beings were at the centre of the cosmos. The pragmatic political philosophy of **Machiavelli** seemed to cut politics free from its traditional link with morality by permitting to statesmen any means which secured the desired end. And the religious movements we know collectively as the Reformation broke with the Church of Rome and set the individual conscience, not ecclesiastical authority, at the centre of the religious life. Nothing, it seemed, was beyond questioning, nothing impossible.

Shakespeare's drama is innovative and challenging in exactly the way of the Renaissance. It questions the beliefs, assumptions and politics upon which Elizabethan society was founded. And although the plays always conclude in a restoration of order and stability, many critics are inclined to argue that their imaginative energy goes into subverting, rather than reinforcing, traditional values. Convention, audience expectation and censorship all required the status quo to be endorsed by the plots' conclusions, but the dramas find ways to allow alternative sentiments to be expressed. Frequently, figures of authority are undercut by some comic or parodic figure. Despairing, critical, dissident, disillusioned, unbalanced, rebellious, mocking voices are repeatedly to be heard in the plays, rejecting, resenting, defying the established order. They belong always to marginal, socially unacceptable figures, 'licensed', as it were, by their situations to say what would be unacceptable from socially privileged or responsible citizens. The question is: are such characters given these views to discredit them, or were they the only ones through whom a voice could be given to radical and dissident ideas? Is Shakespeare a conservative or a revolutionary?

Renaissance culture was intensely nationalistic. With the break-up of the internationalism of the Middle Ages the evolving nation states which still mark the map of Europe began for the first time to acquire distinctive cultural identities. There was intense rivalry among them as they sought to achieve in their own vernacular languages a culture which could equal that of Greece and Rome. Spenser's great allegorical epic poem *The Faerie Queene*, which began to appear from 1590, celebrated

Elizabeth and was intended to outdo the poetic achievements of France and Italy and to stand beside works of Virgil and Homer. Shakespeare is equally preoccupied with national identity. His **history plays** tell an epic story which examines how modern England came into being through the conflicts of the fifteenth-century Wars of the Roses which brought the Tudors to the throne. He is fascinated, too, by the related subject of politics and the exercise of power. With the collapse of medieval feudalism and the authority of local barons, the royal court in the Renaissance came to assume a new status as the centre of power and patronage. It was here that the destiny of a country was shaped. Courts, and how to succeed in them, consequently fascinated the Renaissance; and they fascinated Shakespeare and his audience.

But the dramatic gaze is not merely admiring; through a variety of devices, a critical perspective is brought to bear. The court may be paralleled by a very different world, revealing uncomfortable similarities (for example, Henry's court and the Boar's Head tavern, ruled over by Falstaff in *Henry IV*). Its hypocrisy may be bitterly denounced (for example, in the diatribes of the mad Lear) and its self-seeking ambition represented disturbingly in the figure of a Machiavellian villain (such as Edmund in *Lear*) or a malcontent (such as Iago in *Othello*). Shakespeare is fond of displacing the court to another context, the better to examine its assumptions and pretensions and to offer alternatives to the courtly life (for example, in the pastoral setting of the forest of Arden in *As You Like It* or Prospero's island in *The Tempest*). Courtiers are frequently figures of fun whose unmanly sophistication ('neat and trimly dressed, / Fresh as a bridegroom … perfumed like a milliner', says Hotspur of such a man in *1 Henry IV*, I.3.33–6) is contrasted with plain-speaking integrity: Oswald is set against Kent in *King Lear*.

(When thinking of these matters, we should remember that stage plays were subject to censorship, and any criticism had therefore to be muted or oblique: direct criticism of the monarch or contemporary English court would not be tolerated. This has something to do with why Shakespeare's plays are always set either in the past, or abroad.)

The nationalism of the English Renaissance was reinforced by Protestantism. Henry VIII had broken with Rome in the 1530s and in Shakespeare's time there was an independent Protestant state Church. Because the Pope in Rome had excommunicated Queen Elizabeth as a heretic and relieved the English of their allegiance to the crown, there was deep suspicion of Roman Catholics as potential traitors. This was enforced by the attempted invasion of the Spanish Armada in 1588. This was a religiously inspired crusade to overthrow Elizabeth and restore England to Roman Catholic allegiance. Roman Catholicism was hence easily identified with hostility to England. Its association with disloyalty and treachery was enforced by the Gunpowder Plot of 1605, a Roman Catholic attempt to destroy the government of England.

Shakespeare's plays are remarkably free from direct religious sentiment, but their emphases are Protestant. Young women, for example, are destined for marriage, not for nunneries (precisely what Isabella appears to escape at the end of *Measure for Measure*); friars are dubious characters, full of schemes and deceptions, if with benign intentions, as in *Much Ado About Nothing* or *Romeo and Juliet*. (We should add, though, that Puritans, extreme Protestants, are even less kindly treated: for example, Malvolio in *Twelfth Night*).

The central figures of the plays are frequently individuals beset by temptation, by the lure of evil – Angelo in *Measure for Measure*, Othello, Lear, Macbeth – and not only in tragedies: Falstaff is described as 'that old white-bearded Satan' (*1 Henry IV*, II.4.454). We follow their inner struggles. Shakespeare's heroes have the preoccupation with self and the introspective tendencies encouraged by Protestantism: his tragic heroes are haunted by their consciences, seeking their true selves, agonising over what course of action to take as they follow what can often be understood as a kind of spiritual progress towards heaven or hell.

SHAKESPEARE'S THEATRE

The theatre for which the plays were written was one of the most remarkable innovations of the Renaissance. There had been no theatres or acting companies during the medieval period. Performed on carts and in open spaces at Christian festivals, plays had been almost exclusively religious. Such professional actors as there were wandered the country putting on a variety of entertainments in the yards of inns, on makeshift stages in market squares, or anywhere else suitable. They did not perform full-length plays, but mimes, juggling and comedy acts. Such actors were

THE GLOBE THEATRE,

On the   Bankside.

As it appeared in the reign of King James I.

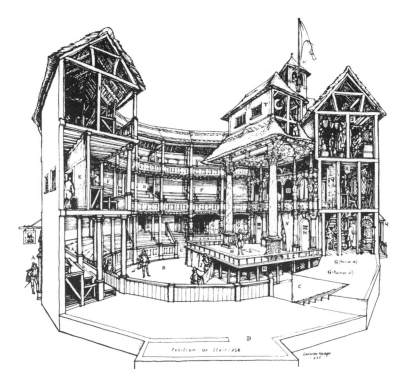

A CONJECTURAL RECONSTRUCTION OF THE INTERIOR OF THE GLOBE PLAYHOUSE

AA Main entrance
B The Yard
CC Entrances to lowest galleries
D Entrance to staircase and upper galleries
E Corridor serving the different sections of the middle gallery
F Middle gallery ('Twopenny Rooms')
G 'Gentlemen's Rooms or Lords Rooms'
H The stage
J The hanging being put up round the stage
K The 'Hell' under the stage
L The stage trap, leading down to the Hell
MM Stage doors

N Curtained 'place behind the stage'
O Gallery above the stage, used as required sometimes by musicians, sometimes by spectators, and often as part of the play
P Back-stage area (the tiring-house)
Q Tiring-house door
R Dressing-rooms
S Wardrobe and storage
T The hut housing the machine for lowering enthroned gods, etc., to the stage
U The 'Heavens'
W Hoisting the playhouse flag

regarded by officialdom and polite society as little better than vagabonds and layabouts.

Just before Shakespeare went to London all this began to change. A number of young men who had been to the universities of Oxford and Cambridge came to London in the 1580s and began to write plays which made use of what they had learnt about the Classical drama of ancient Greece and Rome. Plays such as John Lyly's *Alexander and Campaspe* (1584), Christopher Marlowe's *Tamburlaine the Great* (*c.*1587) and Thomas Kyd's *The Spanish Tragedy* (1588–9) were unlike anything that had been written in English before. They were full-length plays on secular subjects, taking their plots from history and legend, adopting many of the devices of Classical drama, and offering a range of characterisation and situation hitherto unattempted in English drama. With the exception of Lyly's prose dramas, they were in the unrhymed iambic pentameters (**blank verse**) which the Earl of Surrey had introduced into English earlier in the sixteenth century. This was a freer and more expressive medium than the rhymed verse of medieval drama. It was the drama of these 'university wits' which Shakespeare challenged when he came to London. Greene was one of them, and we have heard how little he liked this Shakespeare setting himself up as a dramatist.

The most significant change of all, however, was that these dramatists wrote for the professional theatre. In 1576 James Burbage built the first permanent theatre in England, in Shoreditch, just beyond London's northern boundary. It was called simply 'The Theatre'. Others soon followed. Thus, when Shakespeare came to London, there were theatres, a flourishing drama and companies of actors waiting for him, such as there had never been before in England. His company performed at James Burbage's Theatre until 1596, and used the Swan and Curtain until they moved into their own new theatre, the Globe, in 1599. It was burned down in 1613 when a cannon was fired during a performance of Shakespeare's *Henry VIII*.

With the completion in 1996 of Sam Wanamaker's project to construct in London a replica of the Globe, and with productions now running there, a version of Shakespeare's theatre can be experienced at first hand. It is very different to the usual modern experience of drama. The form of the Elizabethan theatre derived from the inn yards and animal baiting rings in which actors had been accustomed to perform in the past. They were circular wooden buildings with a paved courtyard in the middle open to the sky. A rectangular stage jutted out into the middle of this yard. Some of the audience stood in the yard (or 'pit') to watch the play. They were thus on three sides of the stage, close up to it and on a level with it. These 'groundlings' paid only a penny to get in, but for wealthier spectators there were seats in three covered tiers or galleries between the inner and outer walls of the building, extending round most of the auditorium and overlooking the pit and the stage. Such a theatre could hold about three thousand spectators. The yards were about 80ft in diameter and the rectangular stage approximately 40ft by 30ft and 5ft 6in high. Shakespeare aptly called such a theatre a 'wooden O' in the Prologue to *Henry V* (line 13).

The stage itself was partially covered by a roof or canopy which projected from the wall at the rear of the stage and was supported by two posts at the front. This protected the stage and performers from inclement weather, and to it were secured winches and other machinery for stage effects. On either side at the back of the stage was a door. These led into the dressing room (or 'tiring-house') and it was by means of these doors that actors entered and left the stage. Between these doors was a small recess or alcove which was curtained off. Such a 'discovery place' served, for example, for Juliet's bedroom when in Act IV Scene 4 of *Romeo and Juliet* the Nurse went to the back of the stage and drew the curtain to find, or 'discover' in Elizabethan English, Juliet apparently dead on her bed. Above the discovery place was a balcony, used for the famous balcony scenes of *Romeo and Juliet* (II.2 and III.5), or for the battlements of Richard's castle when he is confronted by Bolingbroke in *Richard II* (III.3). Actors (all parts in the Elizabethan theatre were taken by boys or men) had access to the area beneath the stage; from here, in the 'cellarage', would have come the voice of the ghost of Hamlet's father (*Hamlet*, II.1.150–82).

On these stages there was very little in the way of scenery or props – there was nowhere to store them (there were no wings in this theatre) nor any way to set them up (no tabs across the stage), and, anyway, productions had to be transportable for performance at court or at noble houses. The stage was bare, which is why characters often tell us where they are: there was nothing on the stage to indicate location. It is also why location is so rarely topographical, and much more often symbolic. It suggests a dramatic mood or situation, rather than a place: Lear's barren heath reflects his destitute state, as the storm his emotional turmoil.

None of the plays printed in Shakespeare's lifetime marks act or scene divisions. These have been introduced by later editors, but they should not mislead us into supposing that there was any break in Elizabethan performances such as might happen today while the curtains are closed and the set is changed. The staging of Elizabethan plays was continuous, with the many short 'scenes' of which Shakespeare's plays are often constructed following one after another in quick succession. We have to think of a more fluid and much faster production than we are generally used to: in the prologues to *Romeo and Juliet* (line 12) and *Henry VIII* (line 13) Shakespeare speaks of only two hours as the playing time. It is because plays were staged continuously that exits and entrances are written in as part of the script: characters speak as they enter or leave the stage because otherwise there would be a silence while, in full view, they took up their positions. (This is also why dead bodies are carried off: they cannot get up and walk off.)

In 1608 Shakespeare's company, the King's Men, acquired the Blackfriars Theatre, a smaller, rectangular indoor theatre, holding about seven hundred people, with seats for all the members of the audience, facilities for elaborate stage effects and, because it was enclosed, artificial lighting. It has been suggested that the plays written for this 'private' theatre differed from those written for the Globe, since, as it cost more to go to a private theatre, the audience came from a higher social stratum and demanded the more elaborate and courtly entertainment which Shakespeare's romances provide. However, the King's Men continued to play in the Globe in the summer, using Blackfriars in the winter, and it is not certain that Shakespeare's last plays were written specifically for the Blackfriars Theatre, or first performed there.

R EADING SHAKESPEARE

Shakespeare's plays were written for this stage, but there is also a sense in which they were written *by* this stage. The material and physical circumstances of their production in such theatres had a profound effect upon the nature of Elizabethan plays. Unless we bear this in mind, we are likely to find them very strange, for we will read with expectations shaped by our own familiarity with modern fiction and modern drama. This is, by and large, realistic; it seeks to persuade us that what we are reading or watching is really happening. This is quite foreign to Shakespeare. If we try to read him like this, we shall find ourselves irritated by the improbabilities of his plot, confused by his chronology, puzzled by locations, frustrated by unanswered questions and dissatisfied by the motivation of the action. The absurd ease with which disguised persons pass through Shakespeare's plays is a case in point: why does no one recognise people they know so well? There is a great deal of psychological accuracy in Shakespeare's plays, but we are far from any attempt at realism.

The reason is that in Shakespeare's theatre it was impossible to pretend that the audience was not watching a contrived performance. In a modern theatre, the audience is encouraged to forget itself as it becomes absorbed by the action on the stage. The worlds of the spectators and of the actors are sharply distinguished by the lighting: in the dark auditorium the audience is passive, silent, anonymous, receptive and attentive; on the lighted stage the actors are active, vocal, demonstrative and dramatic. (The distinction is, of course, still more marked in the cinema.) There is no communication between the two worlds: for the audience to speak would be interruptive; for the actors to address the audience would be to break the illusion of the play. In the Elizabethan theatre, this distinction did not exist, and for two reasons: first, performances took place in the open air and in daylight which illuminated everyone equally; secondly, the spectators were all around the stage (and wealthier spectators actually on it), and were dressed no differently to the actors, who wore contemporary dress. In such a theatre, spectators would be as aware of each other as of the actors; they could not lose their identity in a corporate group, nor could they ever forget that they were spectators at a performance. There was no chance that they could believe 'this is really happening'.

This, then, was communal theatre, not only in the sense that it was going on in the middle of a crowd but in the sense that the crowd joined in. Elizabethan audiences had none of our deference: they did not keep quiet, or arrive on time, or remain for the whole performance. They joined in, interrupted, even getting on the stage. And plays were preceded and followed by jigs and clowning. It was all much more like our experience of a pantomime, and at a pantomime we are fully aware, and are meant to be aware, that we are watching games being played with reality. The conventions of pantomime revel in their own artificiality: the fishnet tights are to signal that the handsome prince is a woman, the Dame's monstrous false breasts signal that 'she' is a man.

Something very similar is the case with Elizabethan theatre: it utilised its very theatricality. Instead of trying to persuade spectators that they are not in a theatre watching a performance, Elizabethan plays acknowledge the presence of the audience. It is addressed not only by **prologues, epilogues** and **choruses,** but in **soliloquies**. There is no realistic reason why characters should suddenly explain themselves to empty rooms, but, of course, it is not an empty room. The actor is surrounded by people. Soliloquies are not addressed to the world of the play: they are for the audience's benefit. And that audience's complicity is assumed: when a character like Prospero declares himself to be invisible, it is accepted that he is. Disguises are taken to be impenetrable, however improbable, and we are to accept impossibly contrived situations, such as barely hidden characters remaining undetected (indeed, on the Elizabethan stage there was nowhere at all they could hide).

These, then, are plays which are aware of themselves as dramas; in critical terminology, they are self-reflexive, commenting upon themselves as dramatic pieces and prompting the audience to think about the theatrical experience. They do this not only through their direct address to the audience but also through their fondness for the play-within-a-play (which reminds the audience that the encompassing play is also a play) and their constant use of **images** from, and allusions to, the theatre. They are fascinated by role playing, by acting, appearance and reality. Things are rarely what they seem, either in comedy (for example, in *A Midsummer Night's Dream*) or **tragedy** (*Romeo and Juliet*). This offers one way to think about those disguises: they are thematic rather than realistic. Kent's disguise in *Lear* reveals his true, loyal self, while Edmund, who is not disguised, hides his true self. In *As You Like It*, Rosalind is more truly herself disguised as a man than when dressed as a woman.

The effect of all this is to confuse the distinction we would make between 'real life' and 'acting'. The case of Rosalind, for example, raises searching questions about gender roles, about how far it is 'natural' to be womanly or manly: how does the stage, on which a man can play a woman playing a man (and have a man fall in love with him/her), differ from life, in which we assume the roles we think appropriate to masculine and feminine behaviour? The same is true of political roles: when a Richard II or Lear is so aware of the regal part he is performing, of the trappings and rituals of kingship, their plays raise the uncomfortable possibility that the answer to the question of what constitutes a successful king is simply: a good actor. Indeed, human life generally is repeatedly rendered through the imagery of the stage, from Macbeth's 'Life's but a walking shadow, a poor player / That struts and frets his hour upon the stage / And then is heard no more' (V.5.23–5) to Prospero's paralleling of human life to a performance which, like the globe (both world and theatre) will end (IV.I.146–58). When life is a fiction, like this play, or this play is a fiction like life, what is the difference? 'All the world's a stage ...' (*As You Like It*, II.7.139).

PART SIX

CRITICAL HISTORY & BROADER PERSPECTIVES

STAGE HISTORY

Richard III has always been a popular figure with audiences, who, over several centuries, have thrilled to the compelling story of the rise and fall of the demon king. Shakespeare was not the first writer to deem the last Plantagenet a worthy figure for drama. Thomas Legge's unpublished Latin play, *Ricardus Tertius*, dates from 1579, and there is another anonymous play, *The True Tragedie of Richard III*, which was published in 1594. It seems unlikely that this play pre-dates Shakespeare's *Richard III*, although we cannot be absolutely sure. We do know, however, that *Richard III* was greeted enthusiastically when it was first performed, ranking in popularity with Shakespeare's great **tragedies** *Romeo and Juliet* and *Hamlet*, which were also immediate successes. There is an amusing, possibly apocryphal, anecdote about an early production of *Richard III* starring the celebrated actor Richard Burbage, referred to in the diary of John Manningham, a law student at the Middle Temple. It confirms the popularity of the play and its leading performer:

> Upon a time when Burbage played Richard III there was a [female] citizen grew so far in liking with him, that before she went from the play she appointed him to come that night unto her by the name of Richard III. Shakespeare, overhearing their conclusion, went before, was entertained and at his game ere Burbage came. The message being brought that Richard III was at the door, Shakespeare caused return to be made that William the Conqueror was before Richard III.

Even if this tale is fiction, it surely remains early proof of Richard's seductive power! This anecdote can be found in the New Penguin Shakespeare edition of *Richard III*, edited by E.A.J. Honigmann (1968).

The play was frequently performed up to the time of the English Civil Wars. Thereafter its fortunes languished, following the appearance of a simplified reworking by the actor-playwright Colley Cibber in 1700. Cibber butchered Shakespeare's text, retaining only eight hundred lines, adding a thousand lines of his own and incorporating fragments from other **history plays**. He wanted to focus exclusively on Richard, cutting several roles in order to achieve his aim. Edward IV, Clarence, Hastings and Margaret were all disposed of. Cibber's *Richard III* was enormously popular, succeeding in keeping Shakespeare's play off the stage until Henry Irving presented his own truncated version of the Renaissance text in 1877.

Since the Second World War (1939–45) and the downfall of Hitler, *Richard III* has gained a new lease of life and taken on a new significance for audiences. Its central concern, the machinations of a bloody tyrant, makes it topical for our times. Many directors have used the play to explore ideas about political power, and how it is wielded in totalitarian states. A notable National Theatre production of the 1990s, starring Ian McKellen, portrayed Richard III as a blackshirt fascist in the Oswald Mosley mould. A fine film inspired by this production is readily available on video today, as is an earlier, equally powerful cinematic rendering of the play, directed by and starring Laurence Olivier (1955). Both films are heavily cut versions of the play, but they give viewers a firm sense of Richard's mesmerising and charismatic power.

There is also an engaging film about filming *Richard III* made in 1996 by and starring Al Pacino, *Looking for Richard*. This film includes discussions about the play and its characters, rehearsal scenes and the dramatisation of key moments. It provides a very accessible introduction to the play. A history of the play in performance can be found in the New Cambridge Shakespeare edition of *Richard III*, edited by Janis Lull (1999).

EARLY CRITICAL RESPONSES TO *RICHARD III*

Shakespeare's history plays have attracted less critical attention than his comedies and tragedies. In 1815 John Black translated and published August Wilhelm von Schlegel's *Lectures on Dramatic Art and Literature*. Schlegel took earlier and contemporary critics to task for preferring *Richard III* to the *Henry VI* plays, which, traditionally, had been considered less valuable and interesting than their successor. Like many twentieth-century critics, Schlegel insisted that the *Henry VI* trilogy and *Richard III* should be considered as one ambitious dramatic unit. In *Richard III*, he suggested, Shakespeare was concerned to explore 'the power and the limitations of evil'. In spite of insisting that *Richard III* must be viewed as part of a historical series, Schlegel also saw the play as a tragedy, pointing to Richard's lust for power and the hubris that causes his fall. This critic believed that Shakespeare intended this tragedy to inspire 'terror rather than compassion' in his audiences. Significantly, Schlegel was one of the first to raise doubts about Shakespeare's achievement in *Richard III*, commenting that the anti-hero's 'honourable death ... on the field of battle' was not 'satisfactory to our moral feelings'. Subsequent critics have continued to feel uncertain about the morality of *Richard III*. Schlegel's comments can be found in *Shakespeare's Histories*, edited by Harold Bloom (2000), pp. 14–21.

EARLY TWENTIETH-CENTURY APPROACHES

Eugene M. Waith in *Shakespeare: The Histories* (1965) has suggested that early twentieth-century critics saw Shakespeare's histories as 'interesting failures', inferior to his comedies and tragedies. However, during the 1930s and 1940s a number of scholars undertook research on the history plays. They were seeking to understand Shakespeare's conception of history, and looked at his work in the light of Renaissance models of history and the writings of historians of the period. Two critics were particularly important: Lily B. Campbell and E.M.W. Tillyard. Both considered the relationship between history and theology. Scholars were also interested in Renaissance political theory, and many reached the conclusion that Shakespeare's history plays were conservative in impulse. Briefly, they suggested that Shakespeare's plays confirmed the hierarchical view of the cosmic world order, in which degree must be maintained; if it is not, divine providence will step in to ensure that evil does not triumph over good. There was debate about whether or not *Richard III* could be considered a piece of propaganda, written to serve political purposes. There was – and is – a widely held view that the dramatist accepted and peddled the Tudor myth (see Characterisation and *Richard III* & History). Later critics are divided on this issue. Those who prefer to believe that Shakespeare was not simply slavishly following Richard's Tudor detractors point to the fact that his bad character was not a Tudor invention; by the time Richard III strutted across the boards of the playhouse, audiences were already very familiar with the popular legend of the vicious child-murderer. Elizabethan audiences had specific expectations of the wicked hunchback before they had heard a word of Shakespeare's text.

Twentieth-century critics also commented on the literary/historical sources and dramatic models that Shakespeare turned to when composing his play (see Literary Models & Sources). Discussions about the influence of other writers were closely linked to the ideas outlined in the previous paragraph. Critics were also concerned to define the characteristics and purposes of the history plays as a distinct and separate genre from tragedy. A number noted that this was not a distinction that Shakespeare or his audiences would have made or understood (when it was first published in 1597 *Richard III* was called a tragedy; in the posthumous First Folio of 1623 it appears as a history play). *Richard III* and the *Henry VI* trilogy are discussed in detail in Irving Ribner's 1965 work *The English History Play in the Age of Shakespeare*, while M.M. Reese writes about the origins of the history play in *Shakespeare: The Histories*, edited by Waith (1965), an informative collection of essays that includes work by Campbell and Tillyard.

CONTEMPORARY APPROACHES

Critics have now moved on to new areas of study. *Richard III* has been approached from a variety of different angles, although the ideas outlined above continue to be discussed. Recent commentators, influenced by **feminism, new historicism** and **psychoanalytic criticism,** have shown an interest in the subversive and contradictory elements in the text, in its self-conscious theatricality, and in exploring characters who have been ignored or dealt with cursorily.

Feminist Shakespeareans have considered the roles and functions of the female characters more closely than previous generations, who often characterised the women as feeble and uninteresting victims, wasting few words on them. Janis Lull (see Stage History and Further Reading) argues that Shakespeare uses the female characters to divert sympathy from Richard in the second half of the play, and insists on the power of the lamentation scenes, which have occasionally been dismissed as undramatic and tedious. Bruce W. Young has suggested that the women have power in the play because they seem to be beyond Richard's control, insisting that his mother's vehement curses and refusal to give her son her parental blessing help 'to bring about his downfall'. Recent critics are also interested in sexuality and the way gender roles are presented in the play. Harold Bloom suggests that his sadomasochistic sexuality is the 'crucial component' that makes Richard popular with audiences. His masculine individualism is analysed by E. Pearlman in 'The Invention of Richard of Gloucester' and by I.F. Moulton in 'A Monster Great Deformed: The Unruly Masculinity of Richard III'. Pearlman considers the antagonism between brothers that is a distinct feature of Shakespeare's **history plays**, while Moulton examines the way in which Richard becomes alienated from the 'patriarchal masculine community' when his father dies in *3 Henry VI*. As a result of his inability to mourn his father, Richard's masculine virtues – ambition, bravery of the battlefield, sharp intelligence – are warped and take on a monstrous form, so that Gloucester becomes 'perverse and dangerous to the nation'. Extracts from essays by Young, Pearlman and Moulton can be found in *Shakespeare's Histories*, edited by Bloom (2000). The full text of Young's essay, 'Ritual as an Instrument of Grace: Parental Blessings in *Richard III*, *All's Well That Ends Well*, and *The Winter's Tale*' can also be found in *True Rites and Maimed Rites*, edited by Linda Woodbridge and Edward Berry (1992) on pp. 169–202.

Debates about the subversive nature of the text focus closely on the portrayal of Richard, Richmond and power. Many critics have argued that *Richard III* is a play about playing. Richard's self-conscious theatricality is what draws us in, so much so that some commentators believe it is impossible not to feel a frisson of regret when the great actor dies, regardless of his crimes. Thus Shakespeare's play is subversive: we side with the **Machiavellian** devil, who controls our responses for much of the play through his use of **soliloquies** and **asides**. As Harold Bloom remarks, 'We are on unnervingly confidential terms with him'. This critic draws attention to another feature of the play that makes it potentially subversive: the way in which we are 'entertained by the suffering of others'. Bloom argues that the play is shocking because we are rendered 'incapable of resisting Richard's terrifying charms'. This leaves us in a curious and uncomfortable predicament, unable to fully disassociate ourselves from the villain, and thus unable to fully accept the determinism of the ending. Bloom's comments are taken from his work *Shakespeare, The Invention of the Human* (1998). The chapter on *Richard III* can be found on pp. 64–73.

Richard's godless **irony** also forces us to recognise the inherent ambiguity of language, and the way in which power is constructed through the manipulation of words, which he makes meaningless. Critics have noted the way in which Richard seems simultaneously to subscribe to and subvert the codes of the society he lives in, demonstrating their arbitrary nature. He shows no respect for the community in which he operates. The rituals of birth, marriage and death are treated with contempt. He makes a mockery of the country's laws and ceremonies, and, as William Carroll says in his essay '"The Form of Law": Ritual and Succession in *Richard III*', contaminates 'everything'. Thus the play 'enacts a radical division between the public manifestation of hieratic form and ritual, and the private appetites which undermine and devour them'. Carroll's essay is published in *True Rites and Maimed Rites* (1992) on pp. 203–19. At the same time that he is attacking society's codes, Richard is concerned to be *seen* to uphold the law on numerous occasions, and although he is a usurper himself, he is incensed when challenged by the interloper Richmond. We cannot avoid the conclusion that the play presents us with a number of paradoxical ideas about power. Many would argue that the presentation of the pale and shallow Tudor victor draws our attention to new and potentially subversive doctrines which caused controversy during the Renaissance: the survival of the fittest and the right to overthrow the ruling monarch if he is a tyrant. By focusing on topical issues about the nature of power, and by making his Richard such a vital figure, Shakespeare is perhaps presenting an ambivalent or qualified version of the Tudor myth.

FURTHER READING

EDITIONS OF RICHARD III

Antony Hammond, ed., *King Richard III*, The Arden Shakespeare, Routledge, London, 1988
This is the edition of the text used in the preparation of this Note

E.A.J. Honigmann, ed., *Richard III*, The New Penguin Shakespeare, Penguin Books, Harmondsworth, 1968

> This edition has a readable and informative introduction to the play which deals with its sources, structure, themes and style

Janis Lull, ed., *King Richard III*, The New Cambridge Shakespeare, Cambridge University Press, 1999

> A history of the play in performance can be found in this edition

CRITICISM

The following texts are also useful:

Harold Bloom, *Shakespeare: The Invention of the Human*, Fourth Estate Ltd, London, 1998

> The chapter on *Richard III* can be found on pp. 64–73

Harold Bloom, ed., *Shakespeare's Histories*, Bloom's Major Dramatists, Chelsea House Publishers, Pennsylvania, 2000

Lily B. Campbell, *Shakespeare's 'Histories': Mirrors of Elizabethan Policy*, Huntington Library, San Marino, California, 1947

W.H. Clemen, *The Development of Shakespeare's Imagery*, Methuen, London, 1951

> This includes some helpful comments on the structure and language of the play

W.H. Clemen, *A Commentary on Shakespeare's Richard III*, Methuen, London, 1968

> This offers a detailed scene by scene analysis of the text

Andrew Gurr, *The Shakespearean Stage*, Cambridge University Press, 1980

> An excellent introduction to the history of the Elizabethan playhouses, staging practices and acting companies

Graham Holderness, *Shakespeare: The Histories*, Macmillan Press Ltd, Basingstoke and London, 2000

> Holderness looks at the meaning of the word 'history' and, in a separate chapter on the play, at how history works in *Richard III*. A good introduction to the way criticism of the genre has developed

S.S. Hussey, *The Literary Language of Shakespeare*, Longman, New York, 1982

> There are not many specific comments about *Richard III*, but this is a good introduction to Shakespeare's use of language

L.C. Knights, *Shakespeare: The Histories*, Longman, London, 1962

Madonne M. Miner, "'Neither mother, wife, nor England's queen": the roles of women in *Richard III*' in C.R.S. Lenz, G. Greene and C.T. Neely, eds, *The Woman's Part: Feminist Criticism of Shakespeare*, University of Illinois Press, Urbana and Chicago, 1983

C.W.R.D. Moseley, *Richard III*, Penguin Critical Studies, Harmondsworth, 1989

> An excellent, very comprehensive guide to all aspects of the play

M.M. Reese, *The Cease of Majesty: A Study of Shakespeare's History Plays*, Edward Arnold, London, 1961

Irving Ribner, *The English History Play in the Age of Shakespeare*, revised edition, Methuen, London, 1965

> This gives a detailed discussion of the history play in Shakespeare's time, *Richard III* and the *Henry VI* trilogy

E.M.W. Tillyard, *The Elizabethan World Picture*, Chatto & Windus, London, 1943

Eugene M. Waith, ed., *Shakespeare: The Histories*, Prentice-Hall, Englewood Cliffs, New Jersey, 1965

> This includes the work of Campbell, Tillyard and M.M. Reese, another important Shakespearean scholar, who wrote about the origins of the history play

Linda Woodbridge and Edward Berry, eds, *True Rites and Maimed Rites*, University of Illinois Press, Urbana and Chicago, 1992

> This includes Young's essay, 'Ritual as an Instrument of Grace: Parental Blessings in *Richard III*, *All's Well That Ends Well*, and *The Winter's Tale*' (see pp. 169–202) and William Carroll's essay, "'The Form of Law": Ritual and Succession in *Richard III*' (see pp. 203–19)

HISTORY & BIOGRAPHY

Desmond Seward, *Richard III: England's Black Legend,* Country Life Books, Hamlyn, London, 1983

Alison Weir, *The Princes in the Tower*, Pimlico, London, 1992

Alison Weir, *Lancaster and York: The Wars of the Roses*, Jonathan Cape, London, 1995

World events	Shakespeare's life	Literary events
		1513 Niccolò Machiavelli, *The Prince*
1534 Henry VIII breaks with Rome and declares himself head of the Church of England		**1534** Polydore Vergil, *Urbinatis Anglicae Historiae*
		1543 Thomas More's *History of King Richard the thirde* published
1547 Edward VI accedes to throne		
		1548 Edward Hall's *Union of the Two Noble and Illustre Families of Lancastre and York* published
1553 Mary I accedes to throne		
		1557 More's *History of Richard the thirde* printed fully
1558 Elizabeth I accedes to throne		**1558** Thomas Kyd born
	1564 Born in Stratford-upon-Avon	**1559** George Ferrers, William Baldwin et al., *A Mirror for Magistrates*
1568 Mary Queen of Scots taken prisoner by Elizabeth I		**1564** Christopher Marlowe born
		1572 John Donne and Ben Jonson born
		1576 Erection of first specially built public theatres in London – the Theatre and the Curtain
1577 Francis Drake sets out on round the world voyage		**1577** Raphael Holinshed, *Chronicles of England, Scotland and Ireland*

World events	Shakespeare's life	Literary events
		1579 *Ricardus Tertius*, Thomas Legge's unpublished play, dates from this year
1582 Outbreak of the plague in London	**1582** Marries Anne Hathaway	
	1583 Daughter, Susanna, is born	
	1585 Twins, Hamnet and Judith, born	
	1585-92(c) Moves to London	
1587 Execution of Mary Queen of Scots after implicated in plot to murder Elizabeth I		**1587** First performance of Marlowe's *Tamburlaine the Great;* revised edition of Holinshed's *Chronicles*
1588 The Spanish Armada defeated		
		1589(c) Kyd, *The Spanish Tragedy;* Marlowe, *The Jew of Malta* (not published until 1633)
	1590-3(c) Writes *1–3 Henry VI* and *Richard III*	**1590** Sir Philip Sidney's *Arcadia* and the first three books of Edmund Spenser's, *The Faerie Queene* published
	1590-5(c) Writes *King John*	
1592 Plague in London closes theatres	**1592-4(c)** Probably writes *The Comedy of Errors, Two Gentlemen of Verona, The Taming of the Shrew* and *Titus Andronicus*	**1592** Marlowe, *Doctor Faustus*
		1593 Marlowe is killed in a tavern brawl in Deptford
	1594 onwards Writes exclusively for the Lord Chamberlain's Men	**1594** *The True Tragedie of Richard III* published, author unknown; death of Kyd

World events	Shakespeare's life	Literary events
	1594-5 Writes *Romeo and Juliet, Love's Labour's Lost* and *A Midsummer Night's Dream*	
	1595-6(c) Writes *Richard II*	
	1596 Hamnet dies; William granted coat of arms	
	1596-7 Probably writes *The Merchant of Venice*	
	1597 *Richard III* first published in quarto format	
	1597-8 Writes *1–2 Henry IV*	
	1598-9 Probably writes *Much Ado About Nothing* and *The Merry Wives of Windsor*	**1598** Marlowe's, *Hero and Leander* published
	1599 Buys shares in the Globe Theatre; writes *Julius Caesar, As You Like It* and *Henry V*	
	1600-1 Writes *Hamlet* and *Twelfth Night*	
1601 Essex is beheaded after attempt to overthrow Elizabeth I	**1601** Writes *Troilus and Cressida*	
	1602 Probably writes *All's Well That Ends Well*	
	1602-4 Probably writes *Othello*	
1603 Death of Queen Elizabeth I; accession of James I	**1603 onwards** His company enjoys patronage of James I as the King's Men	**1603** Marston's *The Malcontent* first performed

CHRONOLOGY

World events	Shakespeare's life	Literary events
1604 Peace treaty signed with Spain	**1604** Probably writes *Measure for Measure*	
1605 Discovery of Guy Fawkes's plot to blow up the Houses of Parliament	**1605** First version of *King Lear*	**1605** Jonson, *Volpone*
	1606 Writes *Macbeth*	
	1606-7 Probably writes *Antony and Cleopatra*	
	1607 Writes *Timon of Athens* and *Coriolanus*	**1607** Tourneur's *The Revenger's Tragedy* published
	1608 Writes *Pericles*; the King's Men acquire Blackfriars Theatre for winter performances	**1608** John Milton born
	1609 Becomes part-owner of the new Blackfriars Theatre	
		1610 Jonson, *The Alchemist*
	1611 *Cymbeline*, *The Winter's Tale* and *The Tempest* performed	**1611** King James's translation of the Bible
1612 Last burning of heretics in England	**1612** Retires from London theatre and returns to Stratford	**1612** John Webster, *The White Devil*; Thomas Heywood, *An Apology for Actors*
	1613 Writes *Henry VIII*; the Globe Theatre burns down	
		1614(c) Webster, *The Duchess of Malfi*
	1616 Dies	
1618 Sir Walter Raleigh executed for treason; Thirty Years War begins		
		1622 Molière born
	1623 First Folio published	

allegory (Greek 'speaking otherwise') the simplest form of allegory consists of a story or situation written in such a way as to have two coherent meanings. Any way of understanding a work as containing meanings other than those explicit on the level of its literal surface can be called allegorical

anaphora (Greek 'carrying back, repetition') the rhetorical device of repeating the same words in several successive clauses, often at the start of a line of verse

antanaclasis a pun, in which a word is repeated and its meaning shifted, for example, 'cursed the heart that had the heart to do it'

antithesis (Greek 'opposite placing') opposing or contrasting ideas in next-door sentences or clauses, using opposite or contrasting forms of words. The presentation of arguments in opposition to each other

aside an aside is a common dramatic convention in which a character speaks in such a way that some of the characters on the stage do not hear what is said, while others do. It may also be a direct address to the audience, revealing the character's views, thoughts, motives and intentions

blank verse unrhymed iambic pentameter: a line of five iambs. One of the commonest English metres. It was introduced into England by Henry Howard, Earl of Surrey, who used it in his translation of Virgil's *Aeneid* (1557). Thereafter it became the normal medium for Elizabethan and Jacobean drama. The popularity of blank verse is due to its flexibility and relative closeness to spoken English. It allows a pleasant variation of full strong stresses per line, generally four or five, while conforming to the basic metrical pattern of five iambs

catastasis (Greek 'settlement') the part of the drama in which the action has reached its height

catastrophe (Greek 'overturning') the climactic final moments of a tragedy when the plot is resolved: the tragic denouement

chorus in the tragedies of the ancient Greek playwrights the 'chorus' is a group of characters who represent the ordinary people in their attitudes to the action which they witness as bystanders, and on which they comment. The citizens and the scrivener are obvious choral figures in *Richard III*, while Margaret and the other noble female characters also perform some of the traditional functions of the chorus

closure the impression of completeness and finality achieved by the ending of some literary works

double entendre (French 'hearing twice') from the French term for an ambiguity; often used in English to imply a pun which might have a bawdy or sexual meaning

dramatic irony a feature of many plays: it occurs when the development of the plot allows the audience to possess more information about what is happening than some of the characters themselves have. Characters may also speak in a dramatically ironic way, saying something that points to events to come without understanding the significance of their words. In *Richard III* the villain is both knowingly and unwittingly a figure of irony

epilogue a concluding speech or passage in a work of literature, often summing up or commenting on what has gone before; the epilogue may help to achieve closure

epistrophe (Greek 'a return') the ending of successive clauses with the same word

epitasis the main action of a Greek drama leading to the catastrophe

feminism, feminist feminism is, broadly speaking, a political movement claiming political and economic equality of women with men. Feminist criticism and scholarship seek to explore or expose the masculine 'bias' in texts and challenge traditional ideas about them, constructing and then offering a feminine perspective on works of art. Since the late 1960s feminist theories about literature and language, and feminist interpretations of texts have multiplied enormously. Feminism has its roots in previous centuries; early texts championing women's rights include Mary Wollstonecraft's *A Vindication of the Rights of Women* (1792) and J.S. Mill's *The Subjection of Women* (1869)

foreshadow a technique used to hint at and prepare the reader for later events or a turning point in a work of literature

history play broadly speaking, any play which is set in a historical period. Specifically, however, the term refers to plays which are dramatisations of Holinshed's *Chronicles* of English history (1577, 1587). Shakespeare wrote a large number of history plays, dealing with King John and the complete succession of English kings from Richard II to Henry VII

hubris (Greek 'insolence, pride') the self-indulgent confidence that causes a tragic hero to ignore the decrees, laws and warnings of the gods, and therefore defy them to bring about his or her downfall

humanist originally refers to a scholar of the humanities, especially Classical literature. At the time of the Renaissance, European intellectuals devoted themselves to the rediscovery and intense study of first Roman and then Greek literature and culture, in particular the works of Cicero, Aristotle and Plato. Out of this period of intellectual ferment there emerged a view of man and a philosophy quite different from medieval scholasticism. Reason, balance and a proper dignity for man were the central ideals of humanist thought. The humanists' attitude to the world is anthropocentric: instead of regarding man as a fallen, corrupt and sinful creature, their idea of truth and excellence is based on human values and experience

hyperbole (Greek 'throwing too far') emphasis by exaggeration

image, imagery (Latin 'copy, representation') a critical word with several different applications. In its narrowest sense an image is a word-picture, a description of some visible scene or object. More commonly, however, imagery refers to the figurative language in a piece of literature (metaphors and similes); or all the words which refer to objects and qualities which appeal to the senses and feelings. Thematic imagery is imagery (in the general sense) which recurs throughout a work of art. For example, in *Richard III* images of savage beasts and devils are common, and they are used in such a way as to underpin the play's theme of unnatural evil

irony (Greek 'dissembling') in speech, irony consists of saying one thing while you mean another. Many of Richard's speeches to his victims include examples of irony of this kind. His use of verbal irony is extremely knowing and often incorporates double entendres; for example, he says that he would gladly lend his nephew York his dagger, 'With all my heart' (III.1.111). There is a double irony here: Richard is heartless, and we already know he is scheming against the hapless boy and his brother. Not all ironical statements in literature are as easily discerned or understood; the patterns of irony – of situation, character, structure and vocabulary – in *Richard III* need careful unravelling. In certain cases the context will make clear the true meaning intended, but sometimes the writer will have to rely on the reader sharing values and knowledge in order for his or her meaning to be understood. Ironic literature characteristically presents a variety of

possible points of view about its subject matter. It is possible to argue that
Richard III is in some sense an ironic text: the victor Richmond may be what
England needs, but the audience will simultaneously feel drawn to the glamorous
villain and his wicked ways (see Irony)

Machiavel, Machiavelli a villainous stock character in Elizabethan and Jacobean
drama, so called after the Florentine writer Niccolò Machiavelli (1469–1527),
author of *The Prince* (written 1513), a book of political advice to rulers that
recommended the need under certain circumstances to lie to the populace for
their own good and to preserve power (see Characterisation)

metaphor a metaphor goes further than a comparison between two different things
or ideas by fusing them together: one thing is described as being another thing,
thus 'carrying over' all its associations. When Shakespeare remarks in Sonnet 116
(1609) that love 'is the star to every wandering bark' he defines exactly that
aspect of the star which he wants to associate with love: its constancy and secure
fixedness in a world of change and danger. In *Richard III* the dramatist leaves us
in no doubt about the villain's nature. A number of repellent animal metaphors are
attached to him: hog, boar, toad, spider (see Imagery)

metonymy (Greek 'change of name') the substitution of the name of a thing by the
name of an attribute of it, or something closely associated with it. For example,
'the crown' for the monarchy, 'the stage' for the theatrical profession

new historicism, historicist new historicism refers to the work of a loose affiliation
of critics who discuss literary works in terms of their historical contexts. In
particular they seek to study literature as part of a wider cultural history, exploring
the relationship of literature to society

personification a variety of figurative or metaphorical language in which things or
ideas are treated as if they were human beings, with attributes and feelings

poetic justice Thomas Rymer devised this term in 1678 to describe the idea that
literature should always depict a world in which virtue and vice are eventually
rewarded and punished appropriately. The defeat and death of Richard III is a
prime example of poetic justice at work (see Themes)

prologue the introductory section of a work

protasis (Greek 'proposition, premise') the first part of a dramatic composition

psychoanalytic criticism Freud developed the theory of psychoanalysis as a means
of curing neuroses in his patients, but its concepts were expanded by him and his

followers as a means of understanding human behaviour and culture generally. Literature and creative processes always featured largely in his accounts of the human mind, as both example and inspiration. He asserted that many of his ideas had been anticipated in great literary works, and the terms he devised for his concepts (such as the Oedipus complex) illustrate his reliance on literary models. Critics who adopt a psychoanalytic approach explore the psychological conflicts in texts, seeking to uncover the latent content and psychological realities that underlie the work of art; they look at symbolism and hidden meanings

pun usually defined as 'a play on words': two widely differing meanings are drawn out of a single word, usually for comic, playful or witty purposes. In the sixteenth and seventeenth centuries puns were often used for serious purposes in serious contexts

revenge tragedy a special form of tragedy in which a protagonist pursues vengeance against those who have done wrong. These plays often focus on the moral confusion caused by the need to answer evil with evil. The Elizabethan interest in the tragedies of Seneca gave rise to many examples of this genre. Bloodthirsty scenes, graveyards, ghosts and every kind of sensational horror typify the revenge tragedy from its beginnings

soliloquy (Latin 'to speak alone') a curious but fascinating dramatic convention, which allows a character in a play to speak directly to the audience, as if thinking aloud about motives, feelings and decisions. Many would argue that the use of soliloquies enables the dramatist to give his characters psychological depth. Part of the convention is that a soliloquy provides accurate access to the character's innermost thoughts: we learn more about the character than could ever be gathered from the action of the play alone. In *Richard III* the dramatist uses soliloquies to inform us about Richard's plots, as well as to reveal his character

stichomythia a dialogue carried out in single alternating lines

sub-plot a subsidiary action running parallel with the main plot of a play

synecdoche (Greek 'taking up with, interpreting together') a figure of speech in which a part is used to describe the whole of something, or vice versa. It is common in everyday speech as well as literature, as in the use of 'hand' in the phrase 'all hands on deck' to refer to sailors

tragedy (Greek 'goat song') possibly the most homogeneous and easily recognised genre in literature, and certainly one of the most discussed. Basically a tragedy traces the career and downfall of an individual, and shows in the downfall both the capacities and the limitations of human life. The protagonist may be superhuman, a monarch or, in the modern age, an ordinary person.

Aristotle analysed tragedy in his *Poetics*. He observed that it represented a single action of a certain magnitude, that it provoked in the audience the emotions of pity and terror which were then resolved or dissolved by the catharsis of the play's climax, and that certain features of the plot were common, notably the existence of some connection between the protagonist's downfall and preceding behaviour and the process of 'the reversal of fortune' and the moments of discovery by which the protagonist learnt the truth of his or her situation. Many of Aristotle's ideas are still accepted as valuable insights into the nature of tragic drama.

Seneca was the most influential Roman tragedian; his plays were probably not meant to be performed on stage, though he borrowed his subjects from the Greek playwrights.

In the Middle Ages tragedy was regarded simply as the story of an eminent person who suffers a downfall. The Classical tragedies and theories of Aristotle were unknown.

In English literature the Elizabethan and Jacobean periods are the great age of tragedy. Seneca provided the model both for the formal Classical tragedy with five acts and elaborate style, and for the popular revenge tragedies of blood, full of horrific violent incidents and sensational elements, in which a quest for vengeance leads to a bloodthirsty climax.

Shakespeare's tragedies are characterised by their variety and freedom from convention, in contrast with those of the slightly later Classical revenge tragedians, Racine and Corneille. Shakespearean tragedy concentrates on the downfall of powerful men and often illuminates the resulting deterioration of a whole community around them. The protagonists are not necessarily good: *Richard III* can be considered a punitive tragedy in which evil is justly punished.

Vice, the (Latin 'defect') a figure in morality plays of the fifteenth and sixteenth centuries who tempts mankind in a half-comic, half-unpleasant manner. Many critics claim that Richard is modelled on this stock character (see Characterisation)

Rebecca Warren teaches English. She is the author of York Notes Advanced on *King Lear, Othello, The Taming of the Shrew, The Mayor of Casterbridge* and Sylvia Plath's *Selected Poems*.